Graham W. Hardy

Book Token from Mr & Mrs Mitchell.
Craiglockhart Place.

The Theology of the
Sacraments

D.M.B. aged 60

from a snapshot by S. D. Miller

The Theology of
THE SACRAMENTS
AND OTHER PAPERS

DONALD M. BAILLIE
Late Professor of Systematic Theology
in the University of St. Andrews

with a biographical essay

by

JOHN BAILLIE

FABER AND FABER LTD
24 Russell Square
London

First published in mcmlvii
by Faber and Faber Limited
24 Russell Square London W.C.1
Printed in Great Britain by
Latimer Trend & Co Ltd Plymouth

Contents

Preface

❦

Of the pieces here presented only the short essay on the freedom of the will was written by my brother for publication, and thanks are due to the editors of *The Scottish Journal of Theology* for permission to reprint it. The others were delivered as lectures, and were found among my brother's papers only in the form of lecture notes, fully written out indeed, but written by his own hand with a running pen and quite unrevised. Their style is that of the spoken word, and the contrast between them and the single published essay will at once be apparent. The decision to publish posthumously what an author had himself withheld must always be a delicate and responsible one, but my scruples have been overborne by the many requests reaching me to make available the lectures on the theology of the sacraments which were delivered on the Moore Foundation in the Presbyterian Theological Seminary, San Anselmo, California, in 1952. I have left these (and also the address to Scottish ministers on doctrinal preaching) in their original form, making no attempt to alter their conversational manner, but I have corrected numerous slips of the pen, deleted a few repetitions, adjusted some infelicities of expression such as could only have come from hurried writing, and supplied as many references as I could.

JOHN BAILLIE

9

I

Donald: A Brother's Impression

Donald: A Brother's Impression

❦

The home into which Donald Baillie was born in November 1887 was a Highland manse presided over by a Calvinist divine of strong character and courtly bearing, and a lady of great charm and goodness; but it was saddened by the father's too early death when Donald, the second of three small boys, was only three years old. A year later our mother moved from Gairloch to Inverness, and it was with home and school life in the Highland capital that our earliest significant memories were associated. Our father's Calvinism had been of the most rigorous and uncompromising kind and, true to the memory of a husband with whom she had lived for only six years, our mother was most anxious that her children's upbringing should be in the same tradition. Her own temperament, if left to itself, might have guided her a little differently, and time brought with it a gradual mellowing of principle, especially after the later move to Edinburgh and its University; until finally she felt herself completely at home under Donald's ministry in his various parishes, sharing all his interests and friendships and delighting in them. Nevertheless it was a very rigid Calvinistic outlook with which we were indoctrinated in our boyhood's home. The system of beliefs embodied in the Westminster standards is of a most remarkable logical self-consistency, once its premises have been allowed, and our mother was not only thoroughly conversant with its intricacies, but well able to answer any objections that might be brought

13

against them. If her sons later developed any aptitudes of a philosophic kind, it was undoubtedly by this home training in theological dialectic that their minds were first sharpened.

The sharpening, however, would have been much less, had it not been for our growing doubts about the trustworthiness of some of the premises on which the system rested. These, as I can now see, were first generated in our minds by the considerably different climate of thought to which we were introduced by what we learned at school. None of us was indeed particularly diligent at his set tasks: Donald used to say in after life that he did no work at school. Nevertheless our minds were awakened and our imaginations stirred by what we heard there, and we were given the keys of what to us, brought up as we had been, was something of a new intellectual kingdom—even if our own independent reading and our eager discussions with some of our fellow scholars had as much to do with the actual unlocking of the doors as what our masters (several of whom were very remarkable men) had to tell us. We were indeed fortunate in our schoolmates. I can think of perhaps eight or ten (spread, however, over several forms) who were of the keenest intellectual quality, and the majority of whom have since rendered conspicuous service in Church and University. Donald's own most particular friend was Jack, now Professor J. Y. Campbell of Westminster College, Cambridge, who went up to the University with him and remained his close friend through all his later life. Together we explored the riches of European literature. Together also we served our own apprenticeship in the literary art, especially in the making of what we thought was poetry.

I have often reflected that parents who dutifully bring up their children in a traditional orthodoxy which has never submitted itself to the challenge of Renaissance and *Aufklärung*, and who then send them to a school whose whole ethos is of humanist inspiration, seldom realize the extent of the spiritual stress and strain to which they are thus subjecting them. Our minds, for example, were soon set afire by the reading of Shakespeare, but there was no room at all for Shakespeare within the Puritanism of our early upbringing; no room for theatre of any kind; but especially no room for Shakespeare's large and generous and delicately discriminating appreciation of the human scene. Again, we were trained at school to develop a fastidious sense for the weighing of historical evidence, and for distinguishing fact from legend; but our training at home did not allow us to practise this skill on the Bible stories. Or once more, we were abruptly introduced to the world-view of modern science, and we could not make it square with the up-and-down, three-storey, geocentric universe of the Biblical writers and of our Catechisms, or with their assumptions about the natural history of the human race.

Donald especially was from an early age haunted with religious doubts of this general kind. Having a very sensitive conscience in the matter, he was fearful of unsettling the minds of others by any mention of them, so that it was not until our undergraduate days that I myself was aware of their existence, but I remember how he then said to me, 'If I had only known that your mind had been troubled in the same way, how great would have been the relief of sharing!' For the strain on his spirit was indeed acute. His only confidante was his mother. This may seem surprising in view of what I have already said, but actually it was not so, for the two had from the first been bound together by the closest possible ties of affection and mutual respect. Yet it says much for our mother that she was able to enter so sympathetically and so understandingly into a trouble so remote from anything she herself had ever suffered.

With it all Donald was full of the joy of life, eager to be out of doors as soon as released from school and, in those bicycling days, fond of exploring with a brother or a friend the near-by countryside. Shy and diffident by nature, especially in his approach to strangers, he was none the less full of fun and banter, and had a prettier wit than any of us. His brothers often chaffed him in after life about the remark, couched in the discreet obscurity of the Gaelic language but well enough understood by us, of an old lady who was struck by his failure to enter into the small talk of the hour in my mother's drawing-room: 'Chan 'eil guth aig Dòmhnull.' But the boy thus accused of 'having no voice' was both then and afterwards the life of many a congenial company.

Though so fortunate in our school-fellows, we brothers were probably always one another's greatest friends. In our earliest years we had been thrown all the more closely together by the scrupulous care our mother exercised in the selection of our permitted playmates, though I hasten to add that it was the manners and morals of their homes rather than the social standing of these that controlled her choice. Thus as boys we developed a sort of small-scale 'primitive culture' of our own. We had our own code of *mores*, our own taboos. We invented most of our own games and some of our own romances. We coined innumerable words to denote phenomena and connote shades of meaning for which we did not know the accepted ones. We had our own private names for many lanes and by-ways discovered in our rambles which perhaps nobody had thought it necessary to name before—but they had a significance for some of our games. We had our own names for certain shades of colour, such as 'moon-colour', and Donald and I might on occasion, when we were together, use them until the end of his life. We were interested in identifying the wild flowers, including the weeds in our garden; but we had nobody to tell us their recognized names, nor did we even guess that anybody had ever taken the trouble to name them; so we invented names of our own, many of which I still remember. But there were indeed many regions in which we were similarly forced back on our own resources. We had clearly identified in ourselves and others the innocent presence of a phenomenon which in its psychopathic extremes was afterwards to receive the name of compulsion-neurosis, but our private name for it was 'dooarts', that is, things that one felt one had to do, though without sense or reason, such as touching every second lamp-post as one walked down the street.

When our father died, our mother resolved that all three of her sons should follow in his footsteps as ministers of the Church, though this plan was afterwards so far varied as to

16

encourage the youngest to be a missionary doctor. I cannot remember a time when we did not already know that this was what lay in store for us, nor was there ever a time when we did not, to say the least, accept it without demur. But our mother's resolve was really an astonishing one, since our father, who had never enjoyed more than the minimum ministerial stipend of the day, and who died so soon after marriage, had left her with only the most exiguous of incomes, and since the course of training for the ministry required a minimum of seven years' attendance at the University. But she went forward in faith, no words being more often on her lips than 'The Lord will provide' and 'He will bless the house of Aaron'. She firmly believed that He would; and though she must often have been sorely worried, she not only kept her worries to herself but never allowed them to disturb either her inward peace or her outward demeanour. How she managed I have little notion, and I believe those of her contemporaries who knew her circumstances had even less. I can now see that there was little luxury in our household. I can remember that even in our teens a penny was still a precious coin. But as boys we had no awareness of being poorly off, nor can I believe that we ever lacked anything that we badly needed. Later on, at the University, we had perhaps to deny ourselves certain things that our fellow students (or some of them) were able to enjoy, but I cannot think that we ever felt the deprivation keenly. Yet none of us ever earned a penny until well on in our twenties, apart from the winning of the very valuable competitive scholarships which finally brought great relief. Though we were thrifty enough, we were at an age when money meant little to us, playing almost no part in our thoughts. Donald, indeed, never advanced beyond that age. He just could not bring himself to be interested in the state of his own finances—though we used to tell him that this was because he had never married. In later years I have heard him exclaim impatiently, 'I hate money', when faced with the necessity of some financial transaction or computation on his own account. He never knew the amount of his bank balance, and never cared. His needs were modest, and his conscience prevented him from spending much upon himself, though he was inclined to be prodigal in his contributions to the needs of others.

In 1905 our mother moved to Edinburgh to see us all through the University, and Donald began his studies there in the same year. He very soon added to the circle of his friends some who were to be the intimate associates of a life-time, and the same was true of my brother Peter and myself. Our mother made them all welcome, and there were not many days during the ensuing decade when our little study, and tea-table or supper-table, was not enlivened by the presence of one or more of them. They numbered among them some of the best and ablest men it has ever been my lot to meet. Our eager discussions often continued until long after midnight and, though our 'friendly bowl' was not of the same composition as Alexander Pope's, we enjoyed no less than he 'the feast of reason and the flow of soul'.

It was in his second year of study, and in Pringle-Pattison's course of Logic and Metaphysics that Donald first came into his own as a student, winning the first place and medal in a class numbering several hundred. His earlier interest had been rather in the field of English literature, and indeed this interest never left him. In the same year he won George Saintsbury's prize for poetry, the set subject being 'The Wreck of the *Berlin*', and I still carry in my memory Saintsbury's warm words of commendation. All three of us were still much occupied in writing verses, and I was a competitor that year for the same prize, but won only an honourable mention; I remember saying that, having thus been beaten by a younger brother, I regarded my career as a versifier at an end; which remark, though said in jest, turned out to be true enough. It was our brother Peter who, in the course of his medical studies, remained most faithful to Kalliope and Polyhymnia, and after his tragic death (by drowning in India where he had just joined the staff of a missionary hospital) at the age of twenty-five, a volume of his *Songs and Sonnets* was privately printed. We were, however, greatly stimulated in these juvenile scribblings by the presence in our intimate circle of other versifiers more able than ourselves; notably by Andrew Young, now Canon of Chichester and holder of the Queen's Medal for Poetry, whose numerous volumes are well known to all discerning lovers of the craft; and by Ella Fisher, who lived with us for a year or more, and who published *Pursuit and Other Poems* with Maunsel of Dublin in 1913. But since it is of Donald I am writing, I shall take leave to quote one of the simplest of his early ditties, as I found it among his papers after his death.

> *Life is sweet and death is cold*
> *And, though the world is hard to tread,*
> *The morning glow and sunset red*
> *And earth's bright treasures manifold*
> *Say, Life is sweet and death is cold.*
>
> *Love is warm and hate is chill*
> *And, though the world is strange and proud,*
> *Yet like a rainbow shines the cloud*
> *When eyes and lips and laughter still*
> *Say, Love is warm and hate is chill.*
>
> *Life is sweet and love is warm,*
> *And what of all the woes that come*
> *When winds are loud and birds are dumb?*
> *Forget the woes and, for a charm,*
> *Say, Life is sweet and love is warm.*

One of the finest of Dr. Gilbert Murray's essays bears the title 'Literature as Revelation', and I think that phrase very well expresses the deep concern that guided Donald in his reading of general literature. He was looking always for light upon the meaning of life and for a solution of the intellectual, and fundamentally theological, problems that continued to haunt him. As has been said, however, he very soon began to vest his hopes rather in philosophy. In this field he carried off all the academic honours under the distinguished guidance of Pringle-Pattison, his brother James Seth, R. P. Hardie and Henry Barker. After graduation he acted for some years as Seth's assistant in the department of Moral Philosophy.

Meanwhile his intellectual distress had become greater than ever, as his uncertainties extended to more fundamental issues. I remember his telling me long afterwards of how, as he sat reading a book of apologetic intent by one of the famous preachers of the day, it suddenly came to him that there was no God; and I have often thought of this incident as illustrating the grievous harm that may be done by weak and inconclusive apologetic, or by apologetic of the wrong kind, to young minds that are often keen enough to see where the argument falters, so that, as in this case, it has an effect directly contrary to what was intended. Donald was afterwards to be a valiant defender of the faith, and there are many to testify that his wise counsel was the turning-point in the solution of their own difficulties, but he himself had to pass through a long struggle from which only very slowly was he able to emerge. It brought with it nervous strain of an acute kind. He could not coerce himself to the methodical reading of the texts required for the approaching examinations, but would rather concentrate his thought for hours at a stretch on a single page, or even sentence, in one of them which seemed to promise some possible relief of his problem. And how often did I see him sit for a whole evening, staring at a book but not seeing it, and turning no page of it, while his mind kept reverting in spite of himself to a spiritual predicament concerning which the book had no real enlightenment to offer! He sat the final examination with half the texts unread, so that we feared for his First Class, but what he wrote was apparently enough to convince the examiners of the fine quality of his mind.

Throughout this period he remained not only most regular in his devotions but also most scrupulously conscientious, and even what would seem to some supersensitively so, in his bearing towards and dealing with all those with whom he had to do; scrupulously honourable, unselfish, chaste, truthful. He was fond of testifying afterwards to the great help he received in this matter from that greatest of nineteenth-century preachers, who several generations before had passed through so similar an experience, Robertson of Brighton, and especially from his sermon on 'Obedience the Organ of Spiritual Knowledge'; with its teaching that:

'There are hours, and they come to us all at some period of life or other, when the hand of Mystery seems to be heavy on the soul. . . . Well, in such moments you doubt all—whether Christianity be true: whether Christ was man or God or a beautiful fable. You ask bitterly, like Pontius Pilate, What is truth? In such an hour what remains? I reply, Obedience. Leave those thoughts for the present. Act—be merciful and gentle—honest: force yourself to abound in little services: try to do good to others: be true to the Duty that you know. *That* must be right, whatever else is uncertain. And by all the laws of the human heart, by the word of God, you shall not be left in doubt. Do that much of the will of God which is plain to you, and "you shall know of the doctrine, whether it be of God".'

As his mind developed, Donald came on other thoughts that greatly altered the balance of this one, but without ever really displacing it.

After taking his degree he entered New College, Edinburgh and submitted himself to the regular four years' course of theological study in preparation for the ministry. His struggle for faith was now measurably eased, but certainly not yet a thing of the past. Indeed it was never for him completely a thing of the past. Even in his latest years he had periods of depression, in which life seemed to be emptied of its divine meaning. He was in the poorest possible health then, a martyr to a long-standing asthmatic condition, and the depression was physical as well as mental. He would put to himself and to me the question as to whether the extreme bodily lassitude was the cause or the result, or merely the accompaniment, of the darkness of soul. But one thing was always clear to him—that without God and Christ human life was without significance of any kind, devoid of all interest. He would say, 'When the darkness is on me, I walk down the street, and see people walking aimlessly about, and shops and cars and a few dogs, and it all seems to mean nothing and to matter not at all!' It was Pascal's *misère de l'homme sans Dieu.* Blessedly, such periods of depression were seldom of long duration, and certainly (whatever may be thought about cause and effect) they were always associated with the ebbings of his physical resources. Moreover, this whole side of his experience undoubtedly enabled him to enter most sympathetically and most helpfully into the like experience of a large number of students and others who sought his counsel. Only three or four days before his death, as I travelled to his bedside, a young sick-nurse who sat facing me in the railway compartment told me she was on her way home for a long rest necessitated by her nervous condition; and when I asked her if she knew what brought it on, she answered, 'There has recently been a large number of deaths in our nursing-home, some of them terribly distressing, and I can't stand it now that I've ceased to believe in God'. I recounted this to Donald, and through the fabric of his oxygen tent he said to me, 'How many people feel like that, and how many have spoken just like that to me!'

He and I were fortunate in our friends at New College as we had been in our schooldays and undergraduate years. We had excellent teachers, most of them well known and highly honoured throughout the whole Christian world, and they had much indeed to give us. Yet I think our minds were as much stimulated by our keen discussions among ourselves; in the college theological society which has never since flourished quite as it did in those years before the outbreak of the First World War; but also and equally in long rambles with our chosen friends on the Braid and Pentland Hills, in one another's rooms, and perhaps nowhere more frequently than in our mother's house. To our former discussions which had moved mainly in the field of theism and philosophical theology there was now added the new area of New Testament criticism, and this excited us, I think, no less than the other. Those were the days of 'the return to the Jesus of history', when we hoped to be able, by the methods of modern historical science to penetrate behind the later dogma and tradition of the Church, and even behind the thought of the apostolic age, to the actual and original lineaments of our Lord's life and teaching. All the ablest minds both among our teachers and among our fellow students were caught up into this movement, though none of us, I think, was tempted to follow it to the extremes to which it was being carried in certain other quarters, most notably in the German universities. My brother was later to grow keenly critical of some of the presuppositions of the movement but, as his writings show, he felt that the later reaction against it was often of an equally intemperate kind, and that theology was then in danger of merely ignoring the exigency in which the rise of scientific historiography had placed it and, because it could not clearly see its way out of it, pretending to itself that it did not exist.

Among our fellow students were two very remarkable men who were our constant and almost daily companions, and between whom and Donald there existed the very closest ties of intellectual sympathy and personal affection. Cecil Simpson had come to us with double honours in philosophy and classics from the University of Aberdeen, and we all knew at once that here was one of the rarest souls we were ever likely to encounter. Thirty or forty years afterwards Donald and I would ask ourselves whether we had yet met any other with so fine a philosophic mind joined to so noble a character and so winsome a personality. I possess no more vivid memories than those of an Easter vacation which the three of us spent in Holland, chiefly among the masterpieces of Dutch painting, yet not without long merry evenings in the modest hostelries and many rambles through a countryside which the paintings so faithfully reflected—including a pilgrimage to the little house in Rijnsburg from whose window Spinoza, sitting at the lens-grinding machine which still stands there, looked out and saw all things *sub specie quadam aeternitatis*. On the completion of his theological course Cecil was called to be minister of Moss Street Church, Elgin; but that was in the summer of 1914, and within a year and a half he was applying, in spite of his orders, for a combatant commission. He went to France as an officer in the Seaforths and fell within six months. A slim memorial volume was

printed privately in 1918, containing a long poem ('Memorial
Verses') by Andrew Young and an 'Appreciation' by Donald.
'The personality which thus disappeared from our ken,' my
brother there wrote, 'was a remarkable blend of intellectual
and moral forces, and his friends will ever despair of reproduc-
ing in words what was to them such a vivid thing.' And with
Cecil's name will always be associated that of his close friend
and ours, Ross Husband, whose even briefer career so much
followed the pattern of his own. Feeling a like urge to spare
himself nothing of what so many of his generation had to endure, he went to France as an officer in the Black Watch and
within three weeks was killed in the Battle of the Somme—in
September 1916, more than a year before his friend's death. A
memorial volume by his uncle, Dr. D. M. Ross, was published
by Messrs. Hodder and Stoughton in the following year under
the title *A Scottish Minister and Soldier*, and some of the sentences
there quoted from the letters we wrote to his mother will serve
to indicate the manner of man he was. Cecil wrote, 'I never
knew a better man and never shall. . . . He was a saint, though
one hesitates to apply that much-abused word to him: he was so
human, so unselfconscious, so sane and balanced'. Donald
wrote, 'He was indeed a noble fellow with a pure, unselfish,
simple nature. . . . His death in action is just the final self-
sacrifice of one who was always unselfish'. And I, 'I have never
known a more lovable man than Ross, nor have I ever heard
the word lovable applied so often to any man by his friends as
to him. I have never known so remarkable gifts to be united
with such great humility'. The influence of these two friends of
youth was to leave its deep mark upon us both.

During his theological course Donald spent two long semes-
ters at German universities, one at Marburg under Wilhelm
Herrmann and Adolf Jülicher, the other (in company with Ross
Husband and his sister) in Heidelberg under Ernest Troeltsch
and Johannes Weiss. Of these scholars and thinkers it was Herrmann who impressed him most. He used to say in later life that
Herrmann's *Communion with God* was almost a second Bible to
him in those days, but he would add, 'When I read it now, I

find it difficult, in spite of my continued appreciation of its quality, to understand how it could ever have meant quite so much to me'. Not only had his own mind developed and found new pastures upon which to feed, but the whole climate of Protestant theological thought was to suffer radical change in the years following the end of the War in 1918. Donald's own participation in that conflict was marginal and of brief duration. He too thought it his duty, though then a licentiate of the Church, to volunteer for combatant service, and he duly registered under the Derby Scheme, as I think it was called; but his slender physique, and especially the asthmatic condition with which he had now for many years been troubled, stood in the way. In company with his friend Andrew Young he went to France in 1917 to serve with the Y.M.C.A. in a rest-camp, but even there the conditions proved too severe for him, and after a few months he was invalided home with acute inflammation of the kidneys.

Before going to France he had had his apprenticeship in pastoral work by doing duty in St. Boswells for a friend who, though only recently ordained in that charge, was now in France as an officer in the gunners; but as soon after his return as his doctors would allow him, he sought a parish of his own. This he found in Inverbervie on the Kincardineshire coast, and thither our mother followed him, to be for the second time in her life 'the lady of the manse'. For sixteen years the parish ministry claimed him, first in Inverbervie, then in Cupar, and finally in Kilmacolm; and over all three manses our mother presided until her death (following an accident) in 1932. Unsparingly he gave himself to the duties of his cure. After his death there were found among his papers some six hundred and fifty carefully written sermons, as many or more carefully composed prayers, and a score of manuscript books containing sermon-notes, Bible Class addresses and other lectures. His pastoral oversight of his people was carried through with an equally conscientious diligence, in spite of the strain imposed by his difficult breathing, but in this he was greatly aided by the very full and responsible share our mother assumed in all the congregational activities. During this period he was appointed Kerr Lecturer in Glasgow, and in 1927 the lectures appeared in what was his first considerable publication, *Faith in God and Its Christian Consummation*; but he used to say afterwards that he could not understand how he managed to prepare them in the midst of his parish duties; and he would add that he would never now be able to acquire the range of scholarship which those possessed who had never moved out of academic precincts.

In 1934 he was appointed to the chair of Systematic Theology in the University of St. Andrews, which had honoured him with its doctorate in divinity a year previously, and here he was to remain for the remaining twenty years of his life. He called his house there 'The Crask', the name of the 'brae' at the foot of which stood our father's church and manse in Gairloch, and the name likewise given by our mother to her house in Inverness. It now lacked the latter's gracious presence, but Donald was fortunate in securing a house-keeper of exceptional quality who was wholly devoted to him and remained with him to the end. Thus he was able to indulge in the open hospitality in which he delighted, being greatly aided in this by the proximity of our cousins, Professor and Mrs. W. R. Forrester and their children. He loved to surround himself with young folk, most of whom would naturally be students in the University, but he also had a constant stream of visitors to stay with him—scholars from continental universities (Karl Barth, Paul Tillich, Rudolf Bultmann, Emil Brunner and many another), preachers in the University Chapel, Student Christian Movement secretaries and (during the war years) a number of refugees of different kinds. Donald never married. In his young days, though we had many girl friends in whose company he took the greatest pleasure, he never showed the smallest sign of becoming sentimental about any one of them. No doubt the constant company of his mother and his great devotion to her had at least a delaying effect upon any thought of wedlock, but he would say in middle life, 'I suppose I may get married some day.' Certainly our mother's death left him feeling very lonely, and a distinguished psychiatrist, whom he consulted about the period of depression mentioned above, said to me, 'I think it has a great deal to do with how much he misses his mother'— though at the same time he impatiently pooh-poohed the use of any such jargon as a 'mother fixation' in his case. I remember Donald's writing to me at the time of her death (I was then in America), 'It is not enough that I should face the bereavement with resignation: I am determined that it will leave me no less joyful, or even gay, than I was before'.

During his twenty years in St. Andrews my brother's hold upon his students, their eager reception of his teaching, their dependence upon his counsel, and their love of him, grew ever greater; as did also the respect and strong affection in which he was held by the University community at large and by many of the townsfolk. After the Second World War an ever-increasing number of students from abroad, and especially from the United States, found their way to St. Andrews to study under his direction. One of his American students, Mr. C. B. Ketcham, paid the following tribute in the *Dundee Courier* after his death:

'Many of us have travelled five thousand miles to sit at his feet—we would have travelled twice that distance. . . . His teaching had that mark of profound simplicity which can only be the result of years of strenuous, careful study, yet no student of Professor Baillie's found his scholarship overbearing, harsh, or impersonal. Rather were his lectures marked by gentleness, wit and piety. No question was too insignificant, no personal problem too unimportant for his concern. None of us ever discovered the boundary or depth of so great a heart. We came expecting to be impressed, but we were overawed. We came expecting to be friends, but we were loved.'

One of his former Scottish students, the Rev. Murdo Ewan Macdonald of St. George's West Church, Edinburgh, wrote to *The Scotsman*:

'From the beginning we realized that he was a giant, and so

27

great was our awe of him that we were in danger of regarding
him as an Olympian who dwelt apart. We soon learned that he
was the simplest and friendliest of men, the most hospitable of
hosts, a born story-teller, a genius with children. As the months
passed into years we discovered something else—he was a saint
in whose transparent humility we saw reflected the beauty of
holiness.'

In his later years Donald frequently confessed to me that the
focus of his interest had gradually moved onwards from the
more general problems of what is usually called the philosophy
of religion, such as had formerly occupied him, to the detail of
Christian dogmatics; or at least that he now felt it was the
latter field that must claim most of his attention. The wider
issues were no doubt as present to his mind as they had ever
been, but his increasing clarity concerning them enabled him,
as it were, to pass on to, and to grapple more closely with, the
more advanced doctrines of our faith. This order of going,
however, and the whole intellectual and spiritual experience
that lay behind it, made it inevitable that, in spite of his profound study of and veneration for the traditional theological
systems, he should take nothing from them on trust, but must
work out everything independently for himself. Needless to say,
his ability to do this was at all times dependent on the light he
received from others. There was little in contemporary theological literature, whether Protestant or Roman or Eastern
Orthodox, that escaped his attention, and it was from this
reading that he drew much of his nourishment. But in a sense
in which it is perhaps not true of all writers on these subjects, it
had all to be thought out afresh, and to undergo a process of
metabolism in his own mind, before it could be assimilated by
him—or served up to others. For this reason most of what he
wrote is likely to be of greater service to those who have had to
struggle for their religious beliefs than for those whose minds
have never been thus exercised. It was his endeavour to find as
it were the handle by which each facet of Christian doctrine
could most easily be grasped by the contemporary mind, to

discover the way of presenting it which would best reveal the genuinely and 'existentially' Christian meaning which it had been designed to express and to preserve. He was acutely conscious that traditional terminology was often a barrier to such understanding. He felt also that the historic disagreements between the various confessional divisions of the Christian Church, as well as between conflicting schools of theology, were in no small measure due to the fact that each party had pinned its colours and attached its loyalties to certain phrases and forms of expression which grew to be more and more of an offence to the other party; so that no advance could be made towards a reasonable agreement until the opposing vocabularies were considered afresh, in as great as possible a degree of detachment from the heats of ancient controversy, when perhaps the real concerns enshrined in them would turn out to be much nearer to one another than we had been in the habit of supposing. A great part of my brother's writing and teaching was irenic in this sense.

During these years he gave so much of himself to his students, and to certain other causes which I have still to mention, that he felt little urge to publish; nor would he ever be stimulated in that direction by personal ambition, of which there was very little indeed in his make-up. The only book of any size which he set himself to write in this period was *God Was in Christ*, which at once received wide acclaim throughout the English-speaking world and beyond it, and still enjoys large sales both in Britain and in America. Those who know the book will perhaps recognize in it most or all of the intellectual characteristics of which I have been speaking. The clarity and even simplicity which mark every stage of its argument were distilled from a profound and exhausting labour of thought extending over many years, going back indeed to his student days. He used to say that clarity was the only grace of style for which he ever strove. As *The Times* wrote in its obituary notice on the day following his death:

'The cogency, candour and beautiful clarity of this book

were characteristic not only of all his published work—since the Kerr Lectures of 1927 on *Faith in God and Its Christian Consummation*, which reached, when he was only forty, a finished standard of scholarly homiletic—but of the man himself. Like his own hero of the nineteenth century, F. W. Robertson, Baillie was a successful and open combination of mystic and logician. Neither part would let the other get away with anything: he would always reason closely, but never ceased to be sensitive and deeply religious in the treatment of his themes.'

It was his irenic temper and his concern for Christian unity that prompted him to give so much of his time and thought, especially during the last fifteen years of his life, to the concerns of the ecumenical movement, and especially to the organization which was finally incorporated into the World Council of Churches as its Faith and Order Commission; and it was the same interest that led him during the same period to devote so large a share of his mental energy to questions concerning the Church, its ministry and its sacraments. He took a prominent part in the Edinburgh Conference of 1937; for many years he gave part of his summer vacation to committee meetings in Switzerland and other continental countries, his last important contribution being made at the conference which met at Lund, Sweden, in 1952. This included the preaching of the sermon preparatory to the great celebration of Holy Communion in the Cathedral. Many still speak and write to me about that sermon. I did not myself hear it preached, but I was at the time attending other committees in Denmark, and my wife and I crossed over to Lund for a single afternoon, finding Donald suffering so badly from his asthma that he had to creep rather than walk down the street with us. He had served for a long period as chairman of the sub-commission on Inter-communion, and together with Professor John Marsh he edited the large and important volume bearing that title, which appeared in 1952. When death claimed him, he was serving as convener of the Inter-Church Relations Committee of the Church of Scotland and was one of that Church's representatives appointed to

confer with representatives of the Church of England with a
view to the establishment of closer relations. In an appreciation
contributed to *The Times* after his death, Dr. Rawlinson,
Bishop of Derby wrote:

'It had been hoped that the sensitive, equable and lucid mind
of Donald Baillie would have been available to play its part in
our discussions on future occasions; but, alas, this was not to be.
He has already passed from the broken fellowship of the
Church on earth to the unity in Christ of the Church in the
unseen world.'

Donald always felt very much at home under the ministra-
tions of the Church of England, many of whose leading divines
he numbered among his friends. He was ever loyal to his own
Scottish and Presbyterian tradition; but within that tradition,
from a very early date, and increasingly, his leaning was towards the more liturgical mode. The Christian Year meant
very much to him. To the proper order of worship he attached
the greatest importance, and his own prayers in public were
always prepared with the most scrupulous attention to this. He
shrank from any form of expression, in himself or others, which
(as is unfortunately only too common) represents rather the
particular temperament of the ministrant than the universal
need, or which degenerated into a sentimentality and subjec-
tivity of feeling which he regarded as foreign to the true Christian temper.

There were many other causes into which my brother threw
himself with hardly less zeal. He was long a familiar figure at
student conferences, especially those organized by the Student
Christian Movement, where he would deliver a series of
addresses or act as chaplain. He had from the beginning been
one of the sponsors of the Iona Community, and he sought to
advance its interests in any way he could, influencing a remarkable number of his students to become full members.
During the War years he convened the committee whose duty
it was to keep in touch with the large number of men on active
service who had it in mind, or who might be led, to enter the

ministry of the Church of Scotland; and this entailed an exten-
sive correspondence, including the writing of 'friendly letters'
which were printed or duplicated and sent to such prospective
candidates from time to time. He also took a lead in organizing
various local schemes for the relief of refugees and displaced
persons. In two long summer visits to Germany during the
period of Hitler's ascendancy he had seen something of Nazi
tyranny at close second-hand. His revulsion was extreme,
filling him with the desire to co-operate in aiding its victims,
especially the pastors and the Jews, in any way that seemed
open. A concern for social justice lay very near to the core of
his understanding of the Christian faith. He was zealous not
only for religious but for political and especially economic
freedom; zealous also for equality, not in a doctrinaire understanding of it, but in the sense of the removal of the many un-
justified inequalities with which he felt our society to have
traditionally been burdened. He was thus inclined rather
strongly to the left in his political convictions, about which he
was always outspoken, though refusing to sell out to any single
system of economic doctrine and hesitating to attach any label
to his views. He would say, 'I don't know whether I'm a socia-
list or not, but I do certainly think, etc'.

With it all, however, Donald's was a gay spirit, finding de-
light in simple pleasures. Children were greatly attracted to
him, and many were devoted to him in no common degree. He
knew just how to take them, joining most happily and naturally
in their games and other ploys. He would also sparkle with fun
in many a congenial adult company, sometimes amusing us
with limericks, of which I may be allowed to quote a single
example dating from the early days of Karl Barth's ascendancy
—it was afterwards repeated to its victim, calling forth his hearty
laughter:

> *There was a young thinker called Barth*
> *Who walked by himself quite apart.*
>   *His favourite motto*
>   *Was Blast Rudolf Otto,*
> *And Ritschl was wrong from the start.*

He had always been the wit of our family. From his boyhood he had had a sharp tongue, though his sallies were so wrapped in kindliness as to be robbed of caustic effect. On New Year's Day or the King's Birthday, after a brief glance at the honours list, he would fling down the newspaper in feigned disgust and say, 'Passed over once again!' When at our tea-table my mother would on occasion forget to pour him out a cup, he would announce, 'Patience Competition: First Prize—D. M. Baillie; Second Prize—Job'. Or at the dinner-table he would mildly protest against the appearance of a suet pudding (the eating of which tended to aggravate his asthma) with the rhyme:

> *Eat less suet:*
> *Eat more fru-it.*
> *If you do it,*
> *You won't rue it.*

His spare frame made him very sensitive to cold and, coming into a room that was insufficiently heated, he would exclaim, 'Now we know what the Arctic explorers had to endure'. If ever a family argument threatened to become ill-tempered, he would say, 'This correspondence is now closed—Editor'. I have heard him say frequently how grave a defect he regarded the absence from any man's make-up of a sense of humour, however worthy his other attributes.

Over many years, and until the year before his death, Donald was in the habit of joining my own little household in a continental holiday during the summer vacation—in Savoy or Southern Bavaria, on the Brittany Coast, and latterly on several occasions at Gmunden in the Salzkammergut. We had the jolliest possible time together, exercising ourselves all day on the mountains or on (and in) the water, and reading in the evenings or else playing his favourite game of 'Letterbags', the excellences of which are, I think, known only to a very few. He paid three somewhat extended visits to the United States in response to invitations to lecture in various colleges, but these also he was able to combine with some weeks of badly-needed rest. His last holiday was taken in the Sauerland region of

Germany together with Professor and Mrs. Forrester (my wife and I being in America), but his enjoyment of it was greatly hindered by the increasing emphysema which, developing from his life-long asthmatic condition, brought about his death within a few weeks of his return.

Before returning, however, he travelled to Stuttgart to have talks with Dr. Karl Jellinghaus who had just completed a German translation of *God Was in Christ*. The German publishers of the translation had suggested that he add to it an appendix or extra chapter, bringing the discussion up to date, and having particular reference to the so-called 'demythologising' controversy which was the latest excitement in German theology, and was already arousing widespread interest in other lands. Donald's last writing was the composition of this chapter, which has also been included in new British and American editions of the work, under the title 'Christology and Mythology'. Dr. Rudolf Bultmann, whose writings initiated the controversy, was delighted that this chapter was to be added to a book he so much admired. Here is part of what he wrote to me when the news of its author's death reached him:

'In herzlicher Dankbarkeit denke ich an ihn, den Entschlafenen. Es gehört zu den wichtigsten und eindrucksvollen Begegnungen, dass ich ihn kennen lernen dürfte. Einmal hatten wir die Freude, ihn bei uns in unserem Hause begrüssen zu dürfen, und 1935 und 1949 war ich in St. Andrews bei ihm zu Gaste, und die Stunden des Zusammenseins sind mir unvergesslich. Besonders lebendig ist in meiner Erinnerung ein Abend, als wir in theologischen Gesprächen am Kamin in seiner Wohnung zusammensassen. Er schenkte mir bei jenem Besuch "God Was in Christ", und es ist für mich eine besondere Freude dieses Buch als ein Geschenk zu besitzen. Es is das bedeutendste Buch unserer Zeit über das Thema der Christologie. . . . Es ist vorbildlich in seiner vielseitigen und sachlichen Diskussion mit theologischen und anderen religiösen Anschauungen, vor allem aber in seiner Interpretation der dogmatischen Tradition. In dieser Interpretation, die ich in meiner Terminologie als "existentiale" bezeichnen möchte, fühle ich mich tief mit ihm verbunden und reich gefördert,'[1]

Though clear and alert in mind to the last, Donald did not suspect the extremity of his condition until the day before his death. When he then asked me and I told him, he was in no way disturbed or distressed. He asked only that I should read him the hundred and forty-fifth psalm, and this I did in what, though neither of us knew it, was to be his last conscious hour.

The several hundreds of kind letters which I received held many fine and discerning tributes, and I found it very striking that so large a proportion of the writers were fain to make use of the word 'saint'. I shall not quote any more of these, however, but shall here add extracts from two tributes of a more public kind.

The news of my brother's passing was given to a large ecumenical gathering in Edinburgh by its chairman, Sir Thomas Taylor, the Vice-Chancellor of Aberdeen University, who added (as reported in the press):

'In the great succession of Scottish theologians he stood clearly in the front rank. In the ecumenical movement he was widely known and deeply respected. To all who knew him he was the very pattern of the Christian scholar, uniting great intellectual gifts with a depth of faith and a sanctity of Christian character which only a few can attain.'

---

[1] 'It is with deep thankfulness that I think of him who has now fallen asleep. That I should have been permitted to know him remains as one of the most important and significant of my experiences. On one occasion we had the pleasure of having him stay with us in our house. In 1935 and again in 1949 I was his guest in St. Andrews, and the hours we spent together were such as I can never forget. There stands out in my memory with especial clarity one evening when we sat together in his study in theological discussion. On that occasion he gave me his book *God Was in Christ*, and it is a joy to have that book in my possession as a gift from him. It is the most significant book of our time in the field of Christology. It is a model of versatile and understanding dialogue with other theological and religious outlooks, and above all of interpretation of the dogmatic tradition. In this interpretation, which in my terminology I like to call "existential", I feel myself deeply at one with him, and I have found it richly rewarding.'

At a meeting of the Senatus Academicus of St. Andrews University Dr. T. M. Knox, the Principal and Vice-Chancellor, spoke as follows:

'His acuteness of intellect and the range of his scholarship are enshrined in writings which won international fame for their author and made familiar to theologians in every land the name of his College and University. He was the most loyal of colleagues; and he brought to our counsels an integrity of mind and grasp of principle which commanded widespread respect. For many years he had battled against ill-health, and he was one of those who thought it his duty to labour far beyond his physical strength, whether in teaching or writing or service to his fellow men. He was no recluse; he liked good talk; he had the gift of humour and a cultivated aesthetic taste; and the dignity of our University service owed much to his liturgical sense. Many of us and many of his students knew and loved him as a friend: we have had cause to be grateful to him for sympathy in trouble, for advice in difficulty, for aid in need. But above all, he was a man of saintly character in whose presence anything mean or impure or evil seemed to shrivel away. We are all the richer for having known him and immeasurably the poorer for his loss.'

The wreath placed on his grave by his University bore this inscription:

IN PIAM MEMORIAM DONALDI MACPHERSON BAILLIE .
VIRI DOCTISSIMI . COLLEGAE FIDELISSIMI .
AMICI AMANTISSIMI . ANIMAE SANCTISSIMAE .
PRINCIPALIS ATQUE COLLEGAE CURIALES ET
SENATORII

II

The Theology of the Sacraments

LECTURE I

Sacrament, Nature and Grace

❦

M y choice of the subject of sacramental theology for
these lectures did not arise out of a confidence that
I had something very important to contribute, but
rather out of a perception that something needed to be said or,
more accurately, that there was very great need for hard theological thinking on the subject of the meaning of the sacraments.
In an essay first published nearly thirty years ago Paul Tillich
spoke of 'the death of the sacraments' (I think he must have
borrowed the phrase, for he puts it in quotation marks); and
went on to express the conviction that 'the solution of the problem of "nature and sacrament" is today a task on which the
very destiny of Protestantism depends'.[1]

It is of course true that in certain quarters there has been a
very great revival of sacramental religion. And if we were to
draw a line of distinction between the Catholic and the Protestant, we could not say that the sacramental revival was entirely
on the Catholic side of the line. (Indeed it has become plain in
recent years that the antithesis of Catholic and Protestant is far
from clear and cannot be identified with any denominational
boundaries but cuts right across these boundaries.) And in many
of the Churches of the Reformation tradition there has been
something of a beginning of rediscovery of the sacraments, or
at least a yearning for such a rediscovery and a feeling after it.
Yet in these Churches the rediscovery or the yearning has

[1] Tillich: *The Protestant Era*, 1948, pp. 94, 112.

probably been confined to very limited circles. And even if that phrase 'the death of the sacraments' is an exaggeration, perhaps a fantastic exaggeration, yet does it not contain an element of truth as a description of Christianity in many of our modern Churches?

I myself belong to a Church of the Reformed tradition, and, I must confess, it seems to me that in the tradition in which I have been brought up the sacraments mean very much less to the majority of good Church people than they did to their grandfathers. 'The Communion Season' in Scotland used to be a great and solemn occasion. It might be only twice a year, but it had a dominating importance. But now there is undoubtedly a growing desire for the more frequent communion which from the very beginning was in principle part of our Reformed tradition, and along with this a yearning for a deeper understanding of the sacraments. But the yearning has not carried us very far.

Indeed if the movement for much more frequent communion is to go forward and spread (as I hope it will), we may soon discover that we do not know exactly what we are doing, or why we are doing it, because we do not really possess a theology of the sacraments. Whatever we may have done in other departments of Christian truth in the way of thinking out a theology for the twentieth century, we have not thought out for our time this vital part of our faith and practice.

If that is true of the sacrament of the Lord's supper, it is equally true of the sacrament of baptism. Almost all the Churches continue to regard baptism officially as a regular and vital part of the life of the Church; and yet in almost all the Churches there is either a weakening or a confusion or both as regards the question of its meaning. Even within the Baptist Churches, which traditionally have laid so much stress on believers' baptism as marking a momentous turning-point in the individual religious life, and as safeguarding the conception of the 'gathered Church', there is in some quarters a weakening of conviction and practice. At the same time there is undoubtedly in many different places a new heart-searching on the whole subject, and a fresh interest in the whole question of

Christian initiation, the justification of infant baptism, the relation of baptism to confirmation, and so on.

Thus the subject of the theology of the sacraments is one that is calling loudly for our consideration at the present time.

We are indeed at present witnessing a kind of rediscovery of the treasures of Biblical Theology, which, without driving us in a narrowly 'biblicist' direction, has put new life into our theological thinking. And it might well be thought that this is an augury of new hope for the understanding of the sacraments, and especially for such a deeper and more Christian understanding of them as could draw together those of the Catholic and those of the Protestant tendencies. That may very well be true in the long run.

Yet the help that we shall get in this way may be rather indirect than otherwise. The amount of direct teaching in the New Testament about the sacraments is small, and there is lively controversy in our time as to its real meaning. There are many questions of exegesis that we cannot answer with certainty. Our reconstruction of sacramental theology must rather be based on a deeper understanding of the whole Christian message in the New Testament.

In the first two lectures we are to deal with the general nature of the sacraments and their places in the life of faith. And it will be well to begin by asking the simple question: why should we have sacraments at all? The question is forced upon us not only by the emergence of unsacramental Christianity in such movements as the Society of Friends, but also because there is a quite informal and unformulated tendency to unsacramental Christianity in many quarters of the intelligentsia. Indeed to many modern minds which are very far from rejecting religion there is something surprising in the phenomenon of sacramental practice in the life of the Church. Why should not intelligent and educated Christians be content with the more reasonable and rational elements in public worship, preaching and praying and the reading of Scripture and the expression of praise in musical form? Why should they perpetuate such non-rational practices as the sprinkling of water on

41

the head of an unconscious child or the consuming of tiny quantities of bread and wine to the accompaniment of solemn words?

It is easy to answer: 'We do these things because our Lord has laid them upon us. They are not our inventions, but His commands'. But I hardly need to point out that such an answer is not enough. And it is insufficient not only because it has been widely questioned by modern scholarship whether the words of command and institution of baptism and the Lord's supper are really authentic utterances of Jesus Himself in the days of His flesh. I think myself, and I shall be saying later, that a very good case can still be made out for at least an indirect dominical institution of these two sacraments; and in any case they are both obviously very integral parts of the Christianity of the New Testament. But surely it is not our Christian duty to accept either what Jesus instituted or what the New Testament bequeathed in a spirit of blind and unintelligent obedience. If Jesus instituted these sacraments as the New Testament bequeathed them, we want to know why: otherwise we cannot use them with the understanding that alone can save them from formalism at the best and at the worst from magic. What is there in human nature and human needs and our human situation, what is there in the Christian faith, the Christian Gospel, the Christian salvation, what is there in the nature of the divine grace and its ways of working, to demand this strange visible, tangible expression, in material things and in perceptible actions, which we call sacramental? These are the fundamental questions to which we now come.

A SACRAMENTAL UNIVERSE

This is a phrase that has been used a good deal in recent times, usually to indicate the idea that the sacraments in the specific sense are but concentrations of something very much more widespread, so that nothing could be in the special sense a sacrament unless everything were in a basic and general sense sacramental. This may seem at first to conflict radically with that principle which has been so prominent in Reformed theology, that the existence of a sacrament depends entirely on the word of promise, so that it is not anything in the material element, but entirely the divine Word that can make water or bread and wine sacramental. There is a profound truth in that Reformed principle.

But need it exclude the wider idea of a sacramental universe? Is the divine Word entirely absent from the wider world from which it singles out special elements for a specially sacred use? Is there not a basic reason why material things should be taken by the Word and consecrated to be instruments of divine grace? Do they not lend themselves to such a use because God made them, because they are His creatures?

And have they not in some measure had such a use apart from the Christian sacraments? I am not thinking only of the ceremonial usages of ancient Israel, though a reference to them is not irrelevant. It has never been usual in the Christian Church to confine the term 'sacrament' to the Christian sacraments, but to include also what in the Catholic tradition have regularly been called 'the sacraments of the Old Law'. And Reformed theology has regularly gone even further than the Catholic tradition in ascribing to those Old Testament sacraments the same kind of authority and efficacy as to those of the New Testament. That is, of course, because they were regarded, equally with the New Testament sacraments, as based upon special revelation, ordained by the divine Word, though they were destined to be only temporary and preparatory.

But is it legitimate to extend the use of the term still further, and to find a sacramental element in the ethnic religions? It has even been maintained by some writers that it was from Greek religion that the whole sacramental idea came into early Christianity, and that the religion of the Old Testament was essentially unsacramental. However that may be, it is surely difficult to deny that there is something akin to what we mean by 'sacramental' in most religious traditions, including the most primitive. R. R. Marett, the distinguished anthropologist, has a remarkable volume of Gifford Lectures entitled *Sacra-*

ments of Simple Folk: and it would be perverse to maintain that this is a complete misuse of the term or that there is here no kinship whatever.

Apart, however, from the ethnic religions, we must believe that when Christianity took the common elements of water and bread and wine and made sacraments of them, it was because this universe is the sacramental kind of place in which that can fitly happen; because these elements, these creatures of God, do lend themselves to such a use; and because we men and women, who are another sort of God's creatures, do require in our religion such a use of material things and symbolic actions.

Some writers go still further in developing the connection between nature and sacrament. Dr. Lampert, of the Eastern Orthodox tradition, maintains, as a general basis of the sacraments, that there is something holy and theandric in nature itself, and even that in some mystical sense there is a natural connection between baptism and water.[1] Flemington points out that in all ages and in many lands water has been used in religious lustrations, that this is indeed an 'almost universal practice'.[2] Cullmann quotes Tertullian as maintaining an essential connexion between the Holy Spirit and water ever since at the Creation the Spirit of God brooded upon the waters, and thus baptism with the Holy Spirit naturally uses water.[3] It is very interesting to find an intensely Protestant thinker like Tillich, in his essay on 'Nature and Sacrament', pleading for a rediscovery of nature as a 'bearer and object of salvation'. In this way, he maintains, 'Natural objects can become bearers of transcendent power and meaning, they can become sacramental elements', and 'this is the basis for a Protestant rediscovery of the sacramental sphere'.[4]

At the same time it is most important to notice that both the Eastern Orthodox Lampert and the Protestant Tillich are quite

---

[1] E. Lampert: *The Divine Realm*, 1944, p. 120f.
[2] W. F. Flemington: *The New Testament Doctrine of Baptism*, 1948, p. ix.
[3] Oscar Cullmann: *Baptism in the New Testament*, 1950, p. 13 (quoting Tertullian, *De Baptismo*, Ch. 3.).
[4] Paul Tillich: *The Protestant Era*, pp. 102f.

clear that the symbolic power of nature does not in itself make the sacrament. The relation to the historical divine revelation is necessary to make a real sacrament, and therefore the sacrament speaks only to faith.

There is a very interesting passage in Calvin's *Institutes* in which he bases the Christian sacraments on this broader basis of nature, recognizing that God can take any one of His created elements and use it sacramentally, apart from the sacraments in the narrow and proper sense. As an example he takes the rainbow which, in the Genesis story, was given to Noah and his posterity as a sign and pledge of the mercy and faithfulness of God. Now we in the enlightened twentieth century may very well ask: How can the rainbow really be a pledge of the mercy and faithfulness of God? We can indeed imagine primitive man after a deluge of rain seeing its beautiful spectrum suddenly appearing and stretching across the sky, and taking it as a blessed supernatural portent for his comfort and reassurance; but since we now know the rainbow to be a natural phenomenon of the polarization of light by moisture in the air, how can it prove anything about God at all? Let us not, however, imagine that Calvin was naïve and superstitious about it. With a touch of caustic wit he meets that point. 'If any dabbler in philosophy, in order to deride the simplicity of our faith, contends that such a variety of colours is the natural result of the refraction of the solar rays on an opposite cloud, we must immediately acknowledge it; but at the same time we will deride *his* stupidity in not acknowledging God as the Lord and Governor of Nature, who uses all the elements according to His will for the promotion of His own glory. And if He had impressed similar characters on the sun, on the stars, on the earth, and on stones, they would all have been sacraments to us. . . . Shall not God be able to mark His creatures with His Word, that they may become sacraments, though before they were mere elements?'[1]

Here we have a recognition that because nature is God's and He is its creator, it lends itself to His use, and He can make its

---

[1] *Institutes*, Book IV, xiv, 18.

45

natural elements to speak sacramentally to us; not in the sense of a 'natural theology' which can *prove* the purpose of God from a mere contemplation of nature, but in the sense that God by His Word can use, and therefore we by our faith can use, natural objects, and some (like the rainbow) more naturally than others, as sacramental expressions of His mercy and faithfulness.

It is very much the same thing that we find in our Lord's use of natural objects as instruments of faith. The nature-parables of Jesus seem to be not merely passing illustrations of what He had to say, but something more. They depended on the fact that God is the God of nature, that the whole natural world is His and is fitted to speak to us of Him. Nor does this again mean that in the manner of natural theology we can find God in nature, take the facts of nature as giving us premises from which we can validly deduce God, or truths about God, as our conclusion; but rather that faith can use nature sacramentally. 'Consider the lilies of the field, how they grow; they toil not, neither do they spin: And yet I say unto you, That even Solomon in all his glory was not arrayed like one of these. Wherefore, if God so clothe the grass of the field, which today is, and tomorrow is cast into the oven, shall he not much more clothe you, O ye of little faith?'[1]

If that were regarded simply as a syllogistic argument from the beauty of the wild flowers to the conclusion that there is a God who will take care of each one of us and provide for us, it would obviously be a very precarious argument, and no one ever came to believe and trust in God in just that way. Yet we may be sure that when Jesus uttered these words His mind was going back to moments when He had derived real comfort and strength for His faith from the contemplation of the flowers of the field, and the little birds of the countryside. His faith in God saw God's working, God's love and care, in the natural objects, and drew strength from the sight. To His faith these things became sacramental, just as long before in Israel, some Hebrew believer had looked at a rainbow until to his faith it

[1] Matthew vi, 28–30.

46

became a sacrament of the mercy and faithfulness of God. It
is only when God speaks and awakens human faith that the
natural object becomes sacramental. But this can happen to
material things only because this is a sacramental universe,
because God created all things visible and invisible.[1]

BODY AND SPIRIT

We are endeavouring to clarify in our minds our answer to
the question: Why should we have sacraments at all? One of
the old objections to sacraments is that there is something
unspiritual about the use of such material aids to worship,
and that a truly spiritual religion does not need them. Theo
Preiss wrote as follows in his book *Life in Christ*: 'For the early
Christians the sacraments are much less a victory over the gulf
between spirit and matter—that is what they have become,
alas, through the centuries, whence so many pseudo-problems
and false alternatives—than a conquest of the temporal tension
between the present aeon and that which is to come in Jesus
Christ. Obsessed by the question of the relation between the
living Christ and the elements of bread and wine, we pose the
problem in terms of space rather than time, which are more
Hellenistic than Biblical, as if the eucharist were but a non-
temporal rite actualizing the myth of a mystery religion, and
we are incapable of grasping the fact that the problem must be
viewed less in terms of space than of time.'[2]

At this point it is vital to clarify *the distinction between true and
false spirituality*. What is spirituality? What does the word
'spiritual' mean? It is a New Testament word. But how often
it is used in vague and uncertain ways, and in ways that are
quite false to the New Testament. How often it is used in
antithesis to 'bodily' or 'material', with the implication that
the more 'spiritual' a religion is, the more will it wash its hands
of everything belonging to the bodily and the material. But the
New Testament never uses 'spiritual' (*pneumatikos*) in antithesis

---

[1] On this point cf. the famous passage in Mungo Park's *Journal*.
[2] *Life in Christ* (English translation of *La Vie en Christ*), 1954, p. 91f.

to the bodily (*somatikos*). There is no opposition between spirit and body, for there is even such a thing as a spiritual body (*soma pneumatikon*).

Likewise there is in the New Testament no opposition between the spiritual (*pneumatikos*) and the natural (*physikos*). When our English versions make a distinction between the natural body and the spiritual body, St. Paul's Greek word for 'natural' is not *physikon* but *psychikon*, which means 'pertaining to the *psyche*' as distinct from the *pneuma*. And *psyche* meant the vital principle, the life, so that *soma psychikon* might be translated 'animal body' or even 'body in the biological sense'.

Sometimes also, in the New Testament 'spiritual' (*pneumatikos*) is set in opposition to 'carnal' or 'fleshly' (*sarkikos*). But it is very important to realize that in the thought-world of the Bible, in its vocabulary and in its psychology, the flesh does not mean the body, nor does the distinction between spirit and flesh in any way correspond to our distinction between soul and body. The flesh (*sarx*) means human nature, the whole of it, as one soul-body organism; and especially in the Pauline writings it means *fallen* human nature. But it is not the bodily part of man that is evil in human nature. The carnal is not the bodily. The word *sarkikos* in the New Testament might almost be translated 'human' in antithesis to 'divine'; and the spiritual means that higher realm which is the realm of God's action, that higher element in man which is distinguished from the merely natural biological element and which man does not possess at all except in his relation to God. (On all this see the excellent discussion of Paul's use of 'carnal' by Bishop Lesslie Newbigin in *The Reunion of the Church*, pp. 44f.)

I have sometimes thought that the idea of the 'spiritual' in the New Testament might be best explicated by means of the modern concept of the 'personal'. The *psychikos* and the *sarkikos* are really what belongs to the sub-personal realm. The man whose life is confined to these levels is living a sub-personal life. Relationships which never rise above them are not truly personal relationships at all. And no man is living his true life if he is not living as a real person, in personal communion with other persons, and above all in that basic personal relationship with God which we call religion.

Now if that is what 'spiritual' means, it is vastly important to realize it, for then we can see the difference between the true and the false spirituality. There is then no reason whatever why the true spirituality should renounce the aid of material instruments, 'sensible signs', symbols which we can see with our eyes and touch with our hands; in short, sacraments.

What would really be unspiritual would be that the action of the sacraments should be conceived in a sub-personal way. When people speak of 'sacramental grace' they sometimes betray forgetfulness of the fact that grace is 'a gracious personal relationship'. That is a real danger. That would really be unspirituality. To that point we shall have to return at a later stage in the argument.

My present point is that there need be nothing unspiritual, because there need be nothing impersonal, in the religious use of material elements as 'sensible signs' and thus as instruments of divine grace. In this world it is impossible for a person to express himself at all except through the material—words uttered by the tongue and throat and lips and heard by the ear; words written with ink on paper and perceived by the eye. And persons also communicate with each other by symbolic movements, smiles and gestures, handshakes, linking of arms, and embraces, not to speak of the sexual union of man and wife which may be a very spiritual thing.

Moreover personal relationships may be expressed or created or strengthened also by material objects used as gifts which convey affection and may therefore be treasured as long as life lasts.

But further, personal relationships depend in a still more organic way on our *living together* in a material world. And this means living together in the most material sense, sharing the same house, the same room, the same table, the same meals. For cows and sheep, for cats and dogs, even for the most gregarious animals, a meal is simply a meal, a way of satisfying the instincts of hunger and thirst. But for the human kind, for persons, a meal is a social occasion, a means of fellowship. In all ages the breaking of bread together, the sharing of a common cup, have had a profound spiritual significance, as a means and expression of community. The Psalmist said, 'He who ate bread with me hath lifted up his heel against me',[1] and that was the very depth of treachery, because table-fellowship is something sacred.

And that is true not merely because we are animals (for it is not true on the merely animal level) but precisely because we are more than animals, spiritual beings, body-spirit organisms, persons. Personal relationships have that material basis.

Can the same thing be true, however, of our personal relationship *with God*? Well, let us remember for one thing that the sacraments are not merely matters between the individual and God. They are sacraments of the Church, a visible society, and apart from their social and corporate aspect they cannot be understood at all. St. Augustine says: 'Men cannot be united in any profession of religion, whether true or false, unless they are connected by some communion of visible signs or sacraments.'[2] And Calvin, quoting this, goes on to maintain that even observances found among heathen religions are of this nature. They are, in fact, degenerations of the true sacramental observances appointed by God Himself, and 'though they are fraught with error and superstition, at the same time they furnish an evidence that such external signs are indispensable to a profession of religion'.[3]

But even apart from the corporate aspect, is there any reason why our relationship to God, because it is a spiritual relationship, should have to renounce all material and sensible aids and expressions? 'God is spirit', we read in the Fourth Gospel, 'and they that worship must worship in spirit and in truth.'[4] In its context that saying means that the worship of God cannot be bound to any one particular place, Jerusalem or Gerizim, just as the Bible repeatedly teaches that 'God dwelleth not in temples made with hands'. God has no body, God's presence

---

[1] Psalm xli, 9. [2] *Contra Faustum*, ix, 11.
[3] *Institutes*, Book IV, xiv, 19. [4] John iv, 24.

is never local or spatial, and even His omnipresence does not mean that He occupies every part of space, but indicates rather a spiritual or we might say a personal, relationship to the whole of His creation.

And yet it is impossible for us to dispense with spatial symbols of the divine presence. If we tried to do that we should have to give up the use of words. All our language about spiritual realities is full of spatial metaphor. When we say: 'The Lord is in His holy temple', or 'Lift up your hearts. We lift them up unto the Lord', or 'Come down, O Love divine', or 'Feed me with food divine', we are using spatial and material metaphors, 'up' and 'down' and 'come' and 'feed'. And how can we avoid it, if we are to say anything at all?

We should have to keep silent, adopting the *via negativa* of the extreme mystics; and, after all, that can never be more than a corrective, an occasional reminder that the God whom we worship transcends not only all representation, but even all possible words. That is true; and yet we cannot worship God without words, and we shall impoverish our worship if we try to dispense with all other symbols in the realm of sense— music and gesture and ritual action, standing and kneeling, clasping our hands, closing our eyes. So we need not only the Word but also the sacraments—what St. Augustine calls the *verbum invisibile*, the invisible word.

Tillich has an interesting passage in which he points out that religious symbolism both in the Bible and outside it 'uses seeing, feeling and tasting as often as hearing in describing the experience of the divine presence'.[1] That penetrating remark reminds us of something we are curiously apt to overlook. The 'Word' is a metaphor of revelation through the sense of hearing, and as such it is a symbol, for all words are symbols. But we need also symbols that can be seen and touched and tasted; and so we have the water and the bread and the wine and the actions of the sacraments. All alike, including the spoken word are symbols that are perceived by our bodily senses. Why not? (Cf. C. S. Lewis: 'God likes matter; He invented it'.)

[1] *Systematic Theology*, Vol. I, p. 123.

God is spirit, but we are spirit-body, because God has so created us; and for us, who live in the body, there is nothing unspiritual in the use of material aids, sacramental symbols, so long as we use them in a way which *personalizes* (instead of depersonalizing) our relationship to Him.

FAITH AND GRACE IN THE SACRAMENTS

I have been using the principle that 'spiritual' means personal; and it seems to me that this principle is highly illuminating when we come to think out *how* the sacraments are a means of grace, in what sense they are channels of grace; and the kindred question of the relation of the sacraments to faith, whether their efficacy depends on faith.

It is extremely interesting to notice how in the theology of the twentieth century there has in various quarters been an emphasis on the discovery that the grace of God is simply His personal influence upon us. Doubtless that is fundamentally a return to the New Testament conception, or perhaps an extension and development of it. To the New Testament witness, and above all to St. Paul, grace was simply the free forgiving love and mercy of God.

But, as has often been pointed out, in the Patristic period, and above all in the Middle Ages, grace came to be conceived in a much more mechanical, almost a semi-material way, as a mysterious substance or force that could be 'injected' (infused) into the soul through the sacraments, enabling men to achieve what by nature they could not achieve. This gave rise to all those apparently insoluble problems about the irresistibility of grace, the relation of divine grace to human freedom, the relation of grace to faith, and so forth. And though the Reformers in large measure rediscovered the Pauline conception, yet they did not carry it far enough to solve those problems. But in the twentieth century there has been a notable development of the conception of grace as what Oman called 'a gracious personal relationship', to be thought of on the analogy of the influence of a father upon his child.

It seems to me that this line of thought may be of great importance and service in the thinking out of the many problems of Church and sacrament, and we shall return to this at a later point. At present I wish to apply it to the problem of the relation of grace to faith.

It is often said by Protestants, in opposition to the *ex opere operato* doctrine, that the efficacy of the sacraments depends on the faith of the recipient. But is that quite a safe way of putting it? Does not that suggest that the human part comes first, is prevenient? Would that not be to forget that 'all is of God', that even the faith by which we accept God's grace is itself a gift of God, that it is wrought in us by His grace, and partly *by means of* the sacraments?

Thus instead of saying that sacraments depend on human faith, it seems better to say that sacraments *operate through* human faith. And in order to explicate what that means, I should like to use a very simple and homely illustration.

Let us imagine the case of a small child, a little boy, entrusted to the care of a nursery governess. When she arrives, the little fellow is taken into the room where she is, and left in her care. But she is strange to him, he does not trust her, but looks distantly at this strange woman from the opposite corner of the room. She knows that she cannot do anything with him until she has won his confidence. She knows she has to *win* it. The little boy cannot manufacture it, cannot make himself trust the governess. His faith in her is something which he cannot create—only *she* can create it. And she knows that she cannot create it by forcing it; she has to respect the personality of the child; and to try to take the citadel by storm would be worse than useless, and would produce fear and distrust instead of confidence.

She sets about her task gently, using various means—words, gestures, and smiles, and perhaps gifts, all of which convey something of the kindness of her heart. Until at last the little fellow's mistrust is melted away, she has won his confidence, and of his own free will he responds to her advances and crosses the floor to sit on her knee. Now that her graciousness, using all these means, has created his faith, she can carry on the good work she has begun.

No human analogy is anything like adequate to the relation between God and man. But since we are all but as little children in the things of God, and He is our Father, I believe this simple analogy can illuminate some very old problems. We cannot create our faith in God, we cannot make ourselves trust in Him. Our faith must be His gift, His work, yet not in any mechanical sense, whether in the almost deterministic way suggested in some Calvinistic theology or in the mechanical *ex opere operato* way suggested by some Catholic theology. (Professor Leonard Hodgson has shown how near to each other are these two apparently opposite motifs).

God works faith in our hearts. He bestows on us the gift of faith, by winning us, gaining our confidence, not forcing it. His graciousness overcomes our mistrust, His grace creates our faith, so that when we come to Him, it is really *our* faith, and we come willingly. In order to bring about this end He uses means—words, smiles, gestures, symbolic gifts, which we call sacraments. As Baron von Hügel has written: 'I kiss my child not only because I love it; I kiss it also in order to love it. A religious picture not only expresses my awakened faith; it is a help to my faith's awakening.'[1] All such are 'means of grace', methods employed by the graciousness of God to express and develop a gracious personal relationship between Him and us.

When we think of grace in that personal way, a flood of light falls on many questions of sacramental theology, as we may see at later points in these lectures. And particularly light is shed on the relation of the sacramental system which we call the Church to the historic incarnation in which it took its rise. That question of the relation of the sacraments to the historic facts of the creed, to the actual temporal Christian story, will be the subject of the next lecture.

---

[1] *Essays and Addresses*, First Series, 1921, p. 251.

The Sacraments and Sacred History

☙

All Churches are agreed about the essential connection between the Christian sacraments and the actual historic Jesus, so that the assertion of this connection is part of the very definition of a Christian sacrament. (It may even be true of the sacraments of the Old Testament that in the faith of Israel they were closely connected with the acts of God in history, with the *Heilsgeschichte* of the chosen people; it is certainly true of the Passover and certain other Hebrew religious festivals. But it is true in a new and distinctive way of the Christian sacraments.) The sacraments of the Christian Church are not arbitrary symbols chosen from time to time against the background of a sacramental universe on which I dwelt in the last lecture. They are something more. It has always been regarded as being of their very essence that they go straight back historically to the episode of the incarnation, to the words and works of Jesus Christ in the days of His flesh. In this lecture we have to try to see what is the nature of this connection between the Christian sacraments and the incarnation.

THE DOMINICAL INSTITUTION OF THE SACRAMENTS

How far, and in what sense, is it true that Jesus 'instituted' the sacraments of baptism and the Lord's supper? And why, and in what sense, is that historical question important for the

Christian faith? (A Christian sacrament has regularly been regarded by definition as a sacrament instituted by Christ, and the main reason why the Reformed Churches have usually limited the term to these two sacraments, and refused it to the other five, is because the other five cannot make a good claim to dominical institution.)

There can be no question that the fundamental truth with which we are here concerned is the truth that Christianity is a historical religion, with a historical episode at its very heart. If Christianity were simply a system of general timeless truths, having no essential connection with any historical fact, then it might evolve any number of symbolical rites to meet its changing needs and environments in successive ages, and the number might be indefinitely increased, without any special preference for ancient institutes. But Christianity in its very nature is tied to history, and to a particular episode in history. As it has sometimes been expressed, Christianity is not an imperative but an indicative; and not merely a present indicative or a timeless indicative, but an aorist indicative. It tells of something that once happened.

Christianity is a story, and as I like to put it, it is a story with a plot. It is true that the story is not confined to one period of time. In a sense it runs from eternity to eternity. It begins before the beginning of history and in a super-historical realm, with its chapters about the creation and fall, which must needs use 'mythical' or pictorial language. And its final chapters lie ahead of us beyond the end of history, again in a supra-historical realm, speaking of resurrection and judgement and the world to come, which again can only be described in mythical or pictorial terms. But the middle part of the story runs along a terrestrial track, it is firmly nailed down on the soil of history, running even through your life and mine. And the very central chapter, which gives the clue to the whole plot, is about a definite historical episode, which we call theologically the incarnation of God in Jesus Christ. That is what has been spoken of, in a phrase which is perhaps too much quoted, as the 'scandal of particularity'.

Why has the Bible a unique place and authority for Christians, so that it is impossible either to replace it or to add to it? Why must it have a place that no other book can have? Not because it was written by some occult psychic process, some kind of automatic writing, or even by some kind of inspiration which can be distinguished psychologically from the way in which other books are written. Not because it is an infallible compendium of doctrine, for most of it is not doctrine at all. The real reason is that it is the immediate setting of the historical episode of the 'Word made flesh'. It represents the inner circle of witnesses to that episode. Not, of course, merely in the sense of historical eye-witnesses, but also in the sense of witnesses to the *meaning* of Christ, and that betokens a warm living witness which indeed makes the New Testament a book of unique inspiration. But all this arises ultimately out of the fact of historical propinquity to Jesus Christ. And we ought to remember that, since our eyes never looked upon Jesus in the flesh, we are ultimately dependent on the testimony of those who were eye-witnesses, and that is what is behind the New Testament.

Why must the Church of Christ always be 'apostolic'? It is because the Apostles are those who stand nearest to the historic Jesus, the eye-witnesses whose testimony can never be by-passed. Without it we could know nothing of the historical incarnation at all. That is at least part of the reason why the Church must always be built upon the rock of St. Peter and his fellow disciples; at least part of the reason why the Church, the household of God, must be 'built upon the foundation of the apostles and prophets', as we read in Ephesians[1]—whether the word 'prophets' there means the prophets of the Old Testament or of the New; and it is perhaps the reason why, in the imaginative picture of the Apocalypse, the twelve foundations of the City of God are inscribed with 'the names of the twelve apostles of the Lamb'. All these things are so because Christianity is a historical religion, whose very conception of God is bound up with its story of what God has done 'with a strong hand and with an outstretched arm', and centrally with what

[1] Ephesians ii, 20.

57

He did when He entered into human history in the incarnation. And the Christian sacraments have an inseparable connection with that historical fact.

But how far does the nature of a Christian sacrament depend on the definite institution by Christ of a rite with the intention and injunction that it should be continued in His Church to the end of the world?

That is doubtless an important question for theologians of all schools. But it may seem to be specially vital for the Reformed Churches, because of their distinctive conception of the nature of a sacrament. According to Calvin, it follows from the definition of a sacrament that 'there is no sacrament without an antecedent promise of God, to which it is attached as an appendix, to confirm and seal the promise, and to certify and ratify it to us.'[1] That is Calvin's conception of a sacrament; it is a seal set by God upon a promise. We human beings are weak corporeal creatures, and faith in spiritual realities is difficult for us. Therefore God in His kindness has promised helps in the form of sacraments—definite, visible, tangible elements and actions attached to the word of promise, something that we can see and touch, something that we can *do*, to bring the promise home to us and help us to lay hold of it. (It is almost as if Christ were saying to us: '*Do* this thing, perform this sacred action, repeating to yourself the word of promise, and I will give you the promised grace. So you can assure yourself, and your faith will leap out to receive what I give.') But from this it follows that without the promise, the sign would be an empty sign, just as the seal attached to a document would be useless and meaningless unless the document had a *content*. The seal authenticates the content, and the sacrament confirms the divine promise. But then, where are we if historical criticism should tell us that the sacraments were not definitely instituted by Jesus Christ in the sense of making a promise and attaching a sign with the injunction that the sign was to be performed and the promise claimed? We are bound to face that question. What can we say in reply?

[1] *Institutes*, Book IV, xiv, 3.

I would begin my reply by observing that we must beware of treating the idea of a divine promise in too literal and mechanical a way. The promises of God are not merely a collection of oracles guaranteeing something to us in a future tense, like a legal document, an I.O.U. in black and white on paper, however apt Calvin's simile of the seal attached to the charter may be. God's 'covenant' is something larger and deeper than that. It is given to us above all in Jesus Christ. That includes very centrally the actual words He uttered in the days of His flesh. It must always be a serious concern of theological study to determine exactly what He did say, to distinguish His *ipsissima verba*, so far as is possible, from later interpretations of His teaching or oracles put into His mouth by the tradition. That endeavour must surely always be an important part of New Testament exegesis, for the theological significance of a passage may vary a good deal according to whether or not it is judged to have been actually spoken by the lips of Jesus. Yet this does not mean that everything depends upon our being able to prove that any particular saying was actually uttered by the lips of Jesus. The promises of God are Yea and Amen in Christ Jesus not only when they were literally uttered by His lips but in a much more integral way.

This question of the dominical institution of the sacraments is a little like the question of whether and when and in what sense Jesus 'founded' the Christian Church. Did Jesus found the Church, or was it founded after His departure, perhaps on the Day of Pentecost? If Jesus founded it, when did He do it? Was it at Caesarea Philippi, where after Peter's confession He is reputed to have said: 'On this rock I will build my Church'? Or was it when He called His twelve disciples? These become almost unreal questions when we realize that what really founded the Church (or rather reconstituted the ancient people of God as the New Israel of the Christian Church) was the *whole* episode of what God did in Christ, in His life and words and works, His cross, His resurrection and ascension and the gift of the Spirit at Pentecost—the whole of that mighty work of God. And is not the same thing true in some sense of the

59

origin of the sacraments? If so, then the question of their 'dominical' origin does not in the deepest sense depend on a few isolated texts, or on whether these can be taken as the *ipsissima verba* of Jesus in the days of His flesh.

It seems quite clear that the origins of the sacraments of baptism and the Lord's supper do go back in one form or another not only to the very beginnings of the primitive Church, but also right into the life and ministry of Jesus. As regards baptism, recent scholars have made it appear that this Christian rite is organically connected with our Lord's own baptism by John in the Jordan[1] and with much else that followed in His ministry, as well as with His own attitude to His approaching death, just as in the Pauline teaching it is regarded as a kind of spiritual repetition of His death and resurrection. As regards the eucharist, there can be no question that in essence it goes back to what our Lord did with His disciples in the upper room on the night before His crucifixion, even if there is some uncertainty as to the exact words that He used. And some scholars have maintained that it goes back in some form even further still, to various occasions on which our Lord held communal meals with His disciples. Thus we can confidently regard these two rites not only as sacraments of the New Testament, but as 'dominical' sacraments. Not only are they seals which the New Testament sets upon its promises (which are the promises of God), but they are saved from all arbitrariness by a clear historical connection with the episode of the Word-made-flesh. They have an integral continuity with the incarnation.

But what is the essential nature of their connection with the incarnation? And why, in the last resort, is that so vitally important? Here we must consider an idea which has played a considerable part in sacramental theology.

---

[1] Though this is denied by Schweitzer, who maintains that throughout the New Testament and down to Ignatius the baptism of Jesus is never brought into any kind of connection with Christian baptism. See *The Mysticism of Paul the Apostle*, English translation, p. 234.

THE SACRAMENTS AS AN EXTENSION
OF THE INCARNATION

It is sometimes maintained that the sacraments depend upon the historical episode of the incarnation in a more organic way than Calvin had in mind when he spoke of the promise and the sign. This theory may be roughly expounded as follows. Something wholly new came into the world with Jesus Christ; a quite new contact of God with man, a full outpouring of divine grace, or even 'a higher gift than grace . . . God's presence and His very self, and essence all divine'. The Word was made flesh; God became man and came right into the human situation. That is what we call the incarnation. But that did not last for ever. The days of His flesh soon came to an end. Happy were the eyes that saw these things. But what of all future generations? What are they the better? What indeed, unless some means had been provided by which the new thing should be continued among men on earth for all time to come? And this could only be done through a visible sacramental institution, a channel through which the new stream of divine life should continue to flow down the centuries and be available for all men of all future generations. It must be an institution as visible and as corporeal as was the life of Jesus in the flesh. It must be a continuation of that embodiment, must even have a visible and corporeal continuity with it. Thus nothing could avail but a Church which transmits the supernatural gifts of grace in an unbroken stream conserved through apostolic succession and ordination by laying on of hands. By such an institution the new thing that came into history with Christ is retained on the historical scene for all subsequent generations in a sacramental system which is an 'extension of the incarnation'. According to Bishop Gore, it was the theologian Louis Thomassin (1619–95) who first used such a phrase, and particularly with reference to the real presence in the eucharist; holding that while Christ was with men in the flesh nineteen centuries ago, He is still with men in the flesh when in the miracle of the altar the elements are changed into the body and blood of

Christ. But Jeremy Taylor attributes this expression to 'the Fathers'.[1] Thus Christ who became incarnate when born of Mary and lived the incarnate life on earth in a human body for thirty years has continued ever since to be incarnate on earth in the sacramental institution which is His body, the Church. Father Congar actually expresses this by saying: 'Since John the Baptist, God is incarnate'.[2]

What are we to make of this idea that the Church or the sacramental system is the extension of the incarnation?

By far the most penetrating criticism of the idea known to me is that which is given by Bishop Lesslie Newbigin in his book *The Reunion of the Church*. He maintains that if the idea in that form is taken seriously with all its implications, it becomes quite irreconcilable with the teaching of the New Testament. According to the New Testament the incarnation was an event which took place once for all, a thing which had a beginning and an end. And 'Christ's presence with His Church since Pentecost is in a different manner from His presence on earth "in the days of His flesh".' Moreover the main stress of the New Testament is not upon the incarnation itself (God becoming man or the Word becoming flesh) as if that alone could save us, but upon what we may call the susequent redeeming career of the incarnate Lord—His death, resurrection and ascension, all of which seem to drop into the background when we take the Church as simply the extension of the incarnation. But to go still deeper (and here I am still following Bishop Newbigin's argument), in this whole circle of ideas there has often lurked a serious misunderstanding of what is meant by the incarnation of the Son of God. The phrases 'the law of incarnation' and 'the incarnational principle' are used 'in a way which suggests that by the incarnation a new relationship was set up between spirit and matter'. 'But this is not the case. The incarnation was not an event in which spirit entered into matter. To treat it so is to forsake the biblical doctrine that

---

[1] Quoted by J. E. L. Oulton, *Holy Communion and Holy Spirit*, 1951, p. 164.

[2] M. J. Congar, *Divided Christendom*, 1939, p. 91.

man in his totality as an "ensouled body" is the creation of God; that "matter" and "spirit" are equally His creation and are indissolubly bound together by that fact. It was not that spirit entered into matter, but that the Creator entered into humanity, that the Word became flesh, that God lived a human life and died a human death.'[1] Surely Bishop Newbigin is quite right there, as regards the meaning of the incarnation.

But if so, in what sense is the incarnation continued or extended? Was not the incarnation confined to one limited period of time without any extension? So that Christ is present with us now not in the incarnate way but through the Holy Spirit?

At this point a critic might suggest that with these words we are in danger of shifting into a purely 'spiritual' kind of religion, a quite unsacramental religion of the spirit. And he might also remind us that according to orthodox teaching the Son of God not only became man for a brief sojourn on earth, but continues to be God and man for ever. He not only assumed manhood when He became incarnate, but retains His manhood, lifting up humanity itself in a new union with the divine. And this continuation, this permanence of His manhood, according to orthodox Christian teaching, extends even to His body. Thus the Church has always taught that in *that* sense Christ is still incarnate. It has always regarded His resurrection and ascension as not simply the laying aside of the body and the passing of the soul into the heavenly places but as the exaltation of His glorified body, the 'body of His glory'. St. Paul would certainly apply to Christ's body the words which he wrote about the body of any man who dies in Christ: 'It is sown a natural body, it is raised a spiritual body'—a *soma pneumatikon*.

Yes, but surely St. Paul thought of the glorified spiritual body of Christ as existing not on earth but in heaven, withdrawn from us for a period, until the final *parousia*; so that if Christ is still incarnate, He is not incarnate on earth but in Heaven, in the sense that He is still man, He still has His true human nature, as the Church has always taught. And all this

[1] *The Reunion of the Church*, 1948, pp. 59–63.

would lead not to the idea that the Church is a continuation or extension of the incarnation on earth but rather to the idea that we are now living in an era when the incarnate life is no longer here but in heaven. The days of His flesh on earth came to an end, and we are now living between the period of the incarnation and the day of the final consummation which we call the second coming of Christ. That seems to be the time-scheme which emerges from the New Testament and which would be quite disorganized by the doctrine that 'since John the Baptist, God is incarnate'.

And yet when we have to reckon with the fact that in the New Testament the Church, which we have with us on earth during this interim period, is regarded as the Body of Christ, what exactly is meant? According to Oscar Cullmann, the Church is in the New Testament identified with the spiritual body of Christ: it *is* the *soma pneumatikon*. Is that really the case? Is that what St. Paul means? Would he really agree that God or Christ is incarnate in the Church? We have, of course, to remind ourselves that St. Paul does not speak of 'incarnation'; his vocabulary is different. But apart from vocabulary, Paul undoubtedly regards the presence of Christ with His people in the Church as being of a different kind from His presence on earth in the days of His flesh. And what then does he mean by calling the Church the Body of Christ? Does he mean that, as in the days of His flesh the Spirit of Christ inhabited a human body of flesh and blood, now His Spirit inhabits a spiritual body which we call the Church? So that the relation of Christ to the Church is the relation of soul to body?

It seems to me that if we press that idea and take it as the whole truth, we reap a whole crop of errors and difficulties. When St. Paul in First Corinthians speaks of the Church as the Body of Christ, he is using a figure of speech: doubtless a vastly important and fruitful, even an indispensable and inevitable figure, but yet a metaphor which has to be carefully handled because the same metaphor can be used in different ways. And when we come to Colossians and Ephesians, we find that the figure is used with a most interesting and important difference.

Now it has become almost more than a metaphor, and taken on a new fixity of mystical meaning. But this is the significant difference: now the relation of Christ to the Church is not that of the soul to the body, but rather of the *head* to the body. It is quite a different idea from that of Christ being incarnate in the Church. There is evidently considerable fluidity of conception and imagination; and this becomes still plainer when we notice that the same Epistle to the Ephesians which makes so much of the Church as the Body of which Christ is the Head, also uses the metaphor of the Church as the Bride of Christ, whom He loved and redeemed and cleansed that she might be fit to be His Bride.

If we are to work out soundly the relation of Church and sacraments to the historic incarnation, we must take seriously the New Testament doctrine of the Holy Spirit. This doctrine is wholly dependent on the fact of the historic incarnation of God on earth, but it is also wholly bound up with the idea that that incarnation did not go on for ever, but came to an end, and that since then the divine Presence is with us in a new way through the Holy Spirit working in the Church through Word and sacraments.

That excludes the idea that Christ is actually incarnate in the Church. But of course it also excludes the idea, which sometimes seems to lurk in certain sacramental theologies, that we are concerned with a dead Christ who lived and died long ago and whose grace has to come to us across the centuries as it were through an unbroken sacramental channel. That is an even more fatal way of saying that there is an extension of the incarnation through the ages in the Church and sacraments.

I do not mean that any church or any respectable school of theologians really holds this crude position. But it seems to be implied in the way in which people sometimes talk of the apostolic succession through the laying on of hands of bishops, as if it were a channel through which passes a stream of mysterious substance called grace, flowing through the centuries from the incarnate Christ; a stream that would be lost if there were any break in the succession, or any break in the pipe-line

E   65

that runs through the ages. On this view, at its crudest, the Church with its sacraments becomes a kind of supernatural installation instituted by God for the purpose of transmitting to all future time the grace that came into the world with the incarnation. Such a theory forgets that grace is not a transmissible substance but a living personal relationship; and it also seems to imply a dead Christ whose grace has to be transmitted as it were horizontally through the ages. Whereas we ought to think of the living Christ who is with His people in every age through the Holy Spirit, and who establishes with us through His Church, His Word and His sacraments, that personal relationship which is the very meaning of grace.

Must we then reject the whole idea of the sacramental system as an extension of the incarnation? We have seen its difficulties and dangers, but does it not enshrine an element of truth? Certainly it is important to emphasize the *continuity* between the incarnation and the sacraments. It is of the essence of the Christian sacraments that they could not have existed but for the historical incarnation. They have continuity with it, they point straight back to it, they can only be celebrated in the redeemed community which it created, and only by those who within that community have been set apart in a succession which connects us through the ages with the origins of our religion.

But if we are to be at all true to the New Testament, we must make this continuity, this extension of the incarnation wholly dependent on the Word and the Spirit. That is how the continuity of the institution is maintained. P. T. Forsyth holds that the apostolate died with the Apostles, and that its permanent continuation in the Church is not in the episcopate or in the sacramental system, but in the Scriptures, which constitute the apostolic deposit.[1] Yet the Word is not a timeless deposit of philosophy but the story of an *episode*, and when it is spoken, when the story is told, with the witness of the Church, the Holy Spirit does His work, takes of the things of Christ and gives them to us. Christ is present with us, not incarnate in the

---

[1] *The Church and the Sacraments*, 1917, p. 137f.

Church, but through the Holy Spirit working in the Church by
Word and Sacrament. And it all happens that way because
Christianity is the religion of the incarnation.

THE ESCHATOLOGICAL NATURE OF THE SACRAMENTS

A great deal has been said in recent years—perhaps too
much has been said—about the eschatological nature of the
sacraments, and we must try to see why. The words 'eschatology' and 'eschatological', ugly as they are, have almost become
'blessed words' in theological circles, or at least are in danger
of becoming theological jargon.

All this, of course, has grown out of the new 'eschatological'
interpretation of the teaching of Jesus which was sprung upon
the theological world nearly half a century ago by Johannes
Weiss and Albert Schweitzer. In its extreme form, which
Schweitzer himself called 'thorough-going eschatology', it
came like a bombshell, and upset so many things that it was
something of a theological scandal. But it is an extraordinary
fact that, while failing to make good in its extreme form in the
field of New Testament exegesis, the eschatological idea over-
flowed its banks and watered all the land in a fruitful way,
transforming the theological landscape, making the whole of
theology in all its fields more eschatological than it had been
for a long time. The difference might be expressed figuratively
by saying that whereas fifty years ago the theological landscape
was lighted up by the diffused radiance of a sun shining from
overhead through a mist and making the country look flatter
than it was, now it is rather like a landscape illuminated by the
westering sun near the horizon which casts an evening light on
everything and makes even small eminences stand out in sharp
relief with strong light and shade. That difference, which comes
of a renewed interest in the Last Things, has affected almost
every theological field. It is largely this that has given rise to
the very widespread discussion in our time of the meaning of
history, the Christian interpretation of history. It has also

opened up new approaches to Christology, suggesting that we can understand the real significance of Jesus better if we get away from the endless discussion of divine Persons and natures and try to see Him in the setting of that whole *Heilsgeschichte* which runs on through the story of the Chosen People right up to the final coming of the Kingdom of God, and thus see Jesus as the centre-point of history.

Again, the rediscovery of eschatology has given us a new approach to the whole problem of the future life, helping us to see with clearer eyes the vast difference between the Greek idea of the immortality of the individual soul (with which even Christian theology has often operated) and the Biblical idea of a purpose of God running through the ages leading to a final consummation in which God will give His people eternal life through the resurrection of the dead.

But what especially concerns us in this place is the new light which has been thrown by the rediscovery of eschatology upon the meaning of the Church and the sacraments. It is a comparatively recent thing in theological discussion to speak of the eschatological nature of the sacraments, and it is probably more directly due to the influence of Albert Schweitzer's *Mysticism of Paul the Apostle* than is generally realized. In that work (chapter XI) Schweitzer maintains with great learning and ingenuity that in the period of Christian beginnings, Pauline and pre-Pauline, the sacraments of baptism and the Lord's supper had a *purely* eschatological significance. They derived their whole meaning from the conviction that the final age which heralded the Messianic Kingdom had now arrived, and the coming of the Kingdom itself was imminent. This movement of eschatological expectation began with John the Baptist, and even his baptism had this eschatological significance, as a preparation for the coming Kingdom. To the primitive Christian community the two sacraments were a kind of guarantee of entry into the Kingdom. And according to Schweitzer, this eschatological interpretation continued until the prospect of a return of Christ and a coming of the Kingdom within the lifetime of that first generation began to be extinguished. Then the sacraments came to be interpreted in a different way, and we can see the beginning of this within the New Testament itself.

Schweitzer's argument is important as showing how the sacraments could arise out of a purely Old Testament or Hebrew background, in opposition to the prevalent tendency of the *religionsgeschichtliche Schule* to regard them as having developed in the Hellenistic world on Gentile soil through influences connected with the Greek mystery religions. In this as in other matters Schweitzer doubtless went too far with the purely eschatological interpretation, but here as elsewhere even his extreme views have been fruitful and have led to a widespread rediscovery of that aspect of the sacraments which we have called the eschatological.

As a background to the particular sacraments, theology in our time has begun in a new way to speak of the eschatological nature of the Church, or of the Church as an eschatological entity. What does that mean? It is bound up with the rediscovery that the Christian message is a *Heilsgeschichte*, a sacred story, running on from eternity through history to eternity again, with Christ as its central and determinative point. There is no doubt about the presence of that idea in the New Testament. And it has been worked out by writers like Barth and Cullman so as to yield what we may call a time-scheme, a temporal process divided into successive periods, one of which, the period between the ascension of Christ and His second coming, is the period in which we are living. It is an interim period, the 'time between the times', and it is the 'time of the Church'. It is a period in which we may say that the Kingdom has come (since it came with the coming of Christ) and yet has still to come because the final consummation is not yet. Christ is present with us, yet not in the way in which He was present in the days of His flesh, and again not in the way in which we shall enjoy His immediate presence in the final consummation. In this interim period He is present with us through the Holy Spirit in the Church. And in this interim period the Church is always looking back and looking forward.

That is why the Church needs sacraments. And in both baptism and the Lord's supper, the Church looks both back to the death and resurrection of Christ, which have to be reproduced in us, and forward to the full enjoyment of the Kingdom, of which the Holy Spirit given in baptism is an earnest and seal, and whose messianic banquet we rehearse and anticipate in the sacrament of the Lord's supper.[1] When the Kingdom comes, or when we reach heaven, we shall no longer need sacraments, because we shall have passed *ex umbris et imaginibus in veritatem*, we shall be living in the immediate presence of God, we shall be *in patria*. But meanwhile we are *viatores*, present in the body and absent from the Lord, able to see only 'in a mirror and in a riddle'; and a sacrament is a kind of mirror, the kind of mirror of eternal things required by creatures of flesh and blood in a fallen world which has been redeemed but whose redemption is not yet complete. That is our situation, of which and to which the sacraments speak; and that is why we call them eschatological signs.

Finally, lest we should fall into a fashionable jargon which is remote from the common man, we must in a few words try to relate this to our common life.

Even the most untheological minds know sometimes what it means to feel that we are 'strangers and pilgrims' journeying through a world in which we have to walk by faith and not by sight. We have a certain sense of separation, our fellowship is never complete, or even our reconciliation with each other; and the same is true of our relationship to God.

Our very bodies seem to separate us, and we long for a fuller life in which we should be not disembodied spirits, but in some sense 'all one body' in God, and in which faith and love would be as natural as the air we breathe. We cannot be satisfied with a merely 'spiritual' union. We love the bodies of our friends as well as their souls, and when we are separated from them we long to hear the sound of their voices, to see their faces and familiar gestures, and to feel the touch of their hands.

---

[1] On the eschatological reference of baptism for St. Paul see W. F. Flemington, *The New Testament Doctrine of Baptism*, p. 70ff.

And yet even when we have all these things, we know that our isolation has not been quite overcome. It has been overcome in Christ, and in Him we are all one with God and one with each other; and yet our unity will never be complete until we see God face to face. And thus we stand between looking back and looking forward.

'And I saw the holy city, new Jerusalem . . . and I heard a great voice out of the throne saying: Behold, the tabernacle of God is with men, and He shall dwell with them, and they shall be His people, and God Himself shall be with them and be their God . . . and I saw no temple therein: for the Lord God Almighty and the Lamb are the temple thereof.'[1]

When that comes true, there will be no more need of temples and altars, signs and symbols, services and sacraments. But it has not yet come true; and meanwhile we are creatures of flesh and blood in this spoilt and fallen world, and do need the helps which God in His kindness has provided for us in the sacraments of the Gospel.

[1] Revelation xxi, 2–3, 22.

LECTURE III

The Sacrament of Baptism

⚜

Those who are entrusted with the cure of souls in the pastoral ministry must frequently ask themselves with some misgiving what the sacrament of baptism means to the main mass of Church people who bring their children to be baptized. But indeed a great many ministers must sometimes feel that they themselves have more questions to ask about the meaning of baptism than they are able to answer, and that they are thus not very well equipped to give clear and sound guidance to their people as to what they should believe about this sacrament of the Church. Moreover, if they turn to the theologians for guidance they may find among these also a good deal of confusion; and certainly they will find very lively discussion. There is no doubt that in very diverse quarters, from high Anglicanism to Continental Protestantism there has in recent years been a new consciousness of the problems surrounding this sacrament: questions about the origin and meaning of baptism in the New Testament, about its relation to regeneration and conversion; about its place in the economy of 'Christian initiation' and thus about its relation to confirmation, and most of all perhaps, about the justification of the administration of baptism to infants. All the Churches regard baptism as a regular and unquestionable part of the life of the Church and all are to some extent involved in the prevalent confusion about its meaning; so that on all hands the question is being asked: What are we doing, and why are we doing it, when we administer this sacrament?

72

I believe that a great deal of light can be thrown, and indeed has been thrown, on these questions by a return to the study of the New Testament. And yet it is precisely in this age, in which there has been so notable a rediscovery of New Testament theology, and partly even as a result of it, that the perplexity and questioning about baptism have reappeared in all the Churches. It may be a useful beginning to this lecture if I now point out what some of these difficulties are.

SOME DIFFICULTIES

1. In the first place modern critical study of the New Testament has shaken the confidence with which the Churches used to assert, or even to assume without question, that the sacrament of baptism was definitely instituted by Christ. This is so familiar that I need not dwell on it in detail. The main passages for a definite 'institution' are those at the end of St. Mark and St. Matthew. In the case of St. Mark all scholars are agreed that the familiar ending of the *textus receptus* is not part of the original work. The Matthew passage runs: 'Go ye therefore and make disciples of all the nations, baptizing them into the name of the Father and of the Son and of the Holy Spirit.'[1] But there are strong reasons for holding that the command in that form does not go back to the very earliest days of Christianity. For one thing, it seems plain from the Book of Acts that in the earliest days the baptism practised by the early church was not in the threefold name, but 'into the name of Christ', which should surely be impossible if they had the command with the threefold name behind them. But for another thing, scholars have frequently pointed out that when Eusebius cites this passage, which he often does, he usually—indeed in the large majority of cases—leaves out entirely the command to baptise; which suggests that he was familiar with an earlier and shorter text having no mention of baptism. These are conclusions that would be accepted even by conservative scholars. But the parallel with baptismal rites in the Greek mysteries has led

[1] Matthew xxviii, 19.

73

some scholars to the much more radical contention that the sacrament of baptism developed in Christianity through the influence of its Greek environment, and was unknown in the very earliest days of the Church. Even apart from this extreme view, it is evidently a question that must be faced whether the sacrament of baptism can really claim dominical institution.

2. The second difficulty is a less important one. In all our Western churches except the Baptist, the mode of administration in the modern world is not by immersion but by pouring or sprinkling (and we can hardly imagine anything else becoming general in our modern conditions). And yet the most character-istic teaching about baptism in the New Testament appears to be closely connected with the symbolism of baptism by immer-sion. Recent studies have shown that in New Testament thought baptism was closely connected with the death and resurrection of Christ. It stood for the great spiritual event in which a man, united by faith with the death and resurrection of Christ, dies to himself and the world and rises to newness of life, puts off the old man with his deeds and puts on the new man. Now it is quite plain that baptism by immersion provides a powerful symbolism of that process. The catechumen strips himself of his old clothes and goes down into the depths of the water as if to lose his life by drowning and then rises up out of the water, to live again, washed and cleansed, and puts on fresh clothes. What rich and unforgettable symbolism of putting off the old man and putting on the new! And after all symbolism is a vital part of any sacrament; it is a sensible sign, and only through being that can it be something more. But all that powerful symbolism seems to disappear when for the immersion we sub-stitute a few drops of water sprinkled on the brow. Of what is that an expressive sign or symbol to the catechumen himself or to the worshipping congregation? Can it mean the same to us as baptism did to the Christians of the New Testament?

3. But this leads us to what is the most fundamental problem of all, and this is the one which in recent years has exercised the minds and the pens of so many theologians. In the New Testa-ment baptism seems regularly to mean the baptism of grown

men and women who have heard the gospel and have received it with personal faith and now take the deliberate conscious step of entering the Church of Christ. Whereas in all our Churches except those which are in the Baptist tradition the baptism of adults is the exception, and we normally think of baptism as a rite administered to the infant children of Christian parents at an age when they are quite unconscious of it themselves. Moreover it may well seem that the deepest New Testament interpretation of the meaning of baptism is relevant only to adult or believers' baptism, and could never have been worked out at all if the writers had been thinking mainly of a rite administered to unconscious infants. Such consideration as these have led the world's most famous living Protestant theologian to raise again the question whether the baptising of infants can be justified at all, and whether the Baptists are not after all in the right. (If we came to adopt that view, it would involve a revolutionary change in our whole church life, and so we must face the challenge if we are to take the sacrament of baptism seriously at all.)

These are the problems which beset the sacrament of baptism in the modern world. Let us see how we can deal with them.

CAN WE CONTINUE TO CLAIM THAT BAPTISM IS A DOMINICAL SACRAMENT?

I believe that we can. Anyone who wishes to discover the fresh light upon this question that has emerged from recent New Testament study cannot do better than read Mr. W. F. Flemington's admirable monograph, *The New Testament Doctrine of Baptism*,[1] where a fairly convincing case is made out for the thesis that baptism goes back not only to the very beginning of the Christian Church but to the mind and message and purpose of Jesus Himself. This is quite independent of the disputed verse at the end of St. Matthew's Gospel which enjoins baptism in the name of the Father and the Son and the Holy Ghost. It must be admitted that the use of the threefold name in baptism

[1] London, S.P.C.K., 1948.

was not the usage of the very earliest days. But there is a whole network of evidence against the radical hypothesis that baptism itself did not exist in the earliest days of the Church but developed through Hellenistic ideas and usages when Christianity went out into the Gentile world; and this when connected together gives us all the evidence we need about the dominical origin of the sacrament, whether we feel that it is fitting to use the word 'institution' or not. Let me summarise the main points of it, depending very largely on the work of Flemington.

(a) In every part of the New Testament it appears to be assumed that baptism was the universal and essential gate of entry into the Christian community. There were controversies about many things, but about this there is no sign that there was ever any controversy either among Jewish or among Gentile Christians. It is difficult to account for this unquestioning unanimity unless baptism was known to be a usage that came from Jesus Himself.

(b) It is highly important to remember that the ministry of Jesus Himself was closely connected in its origins with a religious movement which had a baptismal rite at its very centre—the mission of John the Baptist. The mission of John was so inseparably associated with baptism in the Jordan that John himself is known in the New Testament as John the Baptiser. It is noteworthy that Josephus speaks of John the Baptiser—strong evidence that that was how he was generally known even outside Christian circles. It has even been suggested that the Greek word was first coined to describe John. That title could not have originated in the later days when Christian baptism was so familiar a custom, but must be a contemporary title which arose spontaneously and persisted. John's mission could not be thought of apart from baptism.

And the connection between the mission of John and the mission of Jesus is equally indubitable. All the gospels begin the story of Jesus with the story of John. That was 'the beginning of the gospel of Jesus Christ',[1] and the story could not be told without that beginning. For the connection of Christian

[1] Mark i, 1.

baptism with all this we may consult G. W. H. Lampe's *The Seal of the Spirit*, especially Chapter XI. Some, if not all, of the original disciples of Jesus had themselves been baptized by John and came to Jesus from John. In the Fourth Gospel there is even some evidence that they continued baptizing after they had become disciples of Jesus and with His authority. But even if we do not lay too great stress upon that, the connection of the ministry of Jesus with a baptismal rite of repentance and cleansing and initiation is quite plain.

(*c*) Another important and altogether unquestioned fact is that Jesus Himself had Himself baptized by John in the Jordan, and various recent writers have emphasized the close connection between this and the institution of Christian baptism. Karl Barth, in *The Teaching of the Church regarding Baptism*,[2] goes so far as to say that this was really how Jesus instituted the sacrament of baptism. In any case it seems obvious that when the early Christians baptized into the name of the Lord Jesus, their thoughts went back to that incident which in the gospel tradition stood immovably at the beginning of His public ministry—the baptism of Jesus Himself by John in the Jordan. And this in spite of Schweitzer's strongly maintained contention that throughout the New Testament and down to Eusebius Christian baptism is never brought into any kind of connection with the baptism of Jesus.[3]

(*d*) There is further the very notable fact that we find Jesus on two different occasions using the word baptism in speaking of the death which He was to die. 'Can you drink of the cup that I drink of, and be baptized with the baptism with which I am baptised?'[4] And again 'I have a baptism to be baptized with; and how am I straitened till it be accomplished!'[1] Now that might seem to be merely a passing metaphor, but for the remarkable fact that in the thought of the early Church, both in the Pauline and in the Johannine writings, and even to some extent in Hebrews and in I Peter, we find Christian

[1] English translation, p. 18ff.
[2] *Mysticism of Paul the Apostle*, English translation, p. 234.
[3] Mark x, 38.   [4] Luke xii, 50.

baptism closely connected with the death and resurrection of Christ as a solemn rite in which the individual becomes so united with Christ that he dies to sin and rises with a new life. It would seem then that the early Christians understood these sayings of Jesus as more than passing metaphors, and understood them as making a vital connection between the sacrament of baptism and the death of Jesus. Both Flemington[1] and Cullmann[2] make a good deal of this, and regard it as a further reason for carrying this new interpretation of baptism, which gives it a significance far beyond that of John's baptism, right back into the mind of Jesus Himself.

Such is the network of evidence which, quite apart from the doubtful verse at the end of St. Matthew's gospel, gives us reasonable assurance of the dominical origin of the sacrament of baptism in the only sense which is of real theological importance.

HOW FAR DOES THE SYMBOLISM OF BAPTISM DEPEND ON IMMERSION?

I do not think we should spend too much time on that question. Do any of the great Churches attach primary importance to the mode of administration? As Barth has pointed out, it is questionable even in the New Testament whether baptism was always by immersion, since we read of three thousand being baptized together in Jerusalem on the day of Pentecost, and it is difficult to see how in that case immersion could have been possible.[3] It is undoubtedly true that the New Testament makes a great deal of the connection between baptism and Jesus' death and resurrection, and uses the symbolism of the descent into the water and then the emergence as signifying our dying to sin and rising with a new life in Christ. But the death and resurrection motif is by no means the only one pursued in the New Testament in its explication of the meaning of Christian baptism.

---

[1] Op. cit. pp. 25ff.
[2] Oscar Cullmann, *Baptism in the New Testament*, pp. 16–22.
[3] Op. cit. p. 10.

Though it is very important, it is one among others. Another is the motif of *cleansing* which includes both forgiveness of past sin and liberation from the corruption of sin; and of this a sprinkling or pouring would be sufficient symbol, inherited from the Old Testament: 'I will sprinkle clean water upon you, and ye shall be clean.'[1] Yet another motif in the New Testament understanding of baptism is that of the outpouring of the Holy Spirit —perhaps indeed this is the most central of all. And this is symbolized even better by a sprinkling of water than by an immersion. Cullmann believes that the later introduction of the laying on of hands as a symbol of the bestowal of the Spirit was due to the fact that the water-dipping, at any rate when considered apart from the baptism of Jesus, seemed inappropriate for this purpose.[2] When we think the matter out theologically, we see that the dying and rising with Christ, and the cleansing, and the outpouring of the Holy Spirit are not three separate realities at all, but aspects of the same reality. They are all aspects of the *newness*, the *renewal*, of which baptism speaks sacramentally to us; a new life, a new and clean conscience, a fresh start, a new heart, a new spirit.

Moreover the symbolism is connected not only with the great events in the story of Christ from Bethlehem to Pentecost, but also with the whole tradition of Jewish sacred lustration and especially proselyte baptism, which marked a new status with the entry of the individual into the community of the chosen people. So Christian baptism from the first had this meaning of *incorporation into the new Israel*, the Body of Christ which is the Church; and thus meant a new status.

When we remember that it is all of grace, and that grace is essentially a personal relationship between God and man, mediated through Christ in His Church, all these newnesses come together into one, and it is this new beginning which is sacramentally given in the rite of baptism. It was natural in the ancient oriental world to symbolize this by a ritual of immer-

[1] Ezekiel xxvi, 35.
[2] Lampe, p. 69, who refers to Cullmann's article in *Rev. de Phil. et Theol.* 30, pp. 121ff.

sion, but is that so natural in the modern Western world? May not the sprinkling be a fitter symbol?

It may indeed be true that in the case of adult baptism a total immersion is calculated to have a far more powerful *psychological* effect both on the person baptized and on the congregation. And it would be foolish to discount the psychological aspect altogether; for whatever else a sacrament may be, it is a ritual in which symbolical elements and actions have an effect upon the mind, communicating to it certain realities which cannot be communicated in words alone. If we denied this we should be in danger of running into magic. Yet on the other hand it is salutary to reflect that a *powerful psychological effect at the moment* is not what matters, and a reliance on emotion may be as dangerous as a lapse into magical ideas. What matters is not momentary emotion but intention and faith.

So we are driven deeper into the whole question of the theology of baptism and I believe the best method of getting deep into that question is by plunging now into the problem which has again become so controversial in our time—whether baptism ought to be administered to infants or only to adult believers.

INFANT BAPTISM OR BELIEVERS' BAPTISM?

We might never get any further with this controversy if we began with the question of the relation between baptism and regeneration. Therefore we will begin with a principle which is accepted by all churches, those which only practise 'believers' baptism' as well as those which practise infant baptism; that *baptism marks the entry of the individual into the community of the church of Christ on earth.* The Baptist theologian, Dr. Wheeler Robinson, in his book on *Baptist Principles*[1] says that 'baptism is the door of entrance to the church'. But if this is accepted, then surely the determinative question about infant baptism must be: *Are the children of Christians to be regarded as having a place within the Church of Christ or are they outsiders?* Those

[1] P. 25.

who deny baptism to infants would seem to be logically in-volved in saying that children are no part of the Church. But the central tradition of reformed Christianity has consistently given the opposite answer, asserting that the Church consists of all professing believers *together with their children*.

So the question comes to be whether this is sound and Christian. Ought we to regard children as part of the Church? Or, to put it more concretely: *Is there such a thing as a Christian child?* This does not mean a perfect child, for even the most mature Christian on earth is not perfect. And it does not mean a child who has passed through an experience of conversion. We shall all agree that it would be unnatural and harmful to try to force upon little children the kind of conversion experi-ence which is common in adolescent or in adult life. But if that is not to be expected or encouraged, how ought the Church to regard and to treat its children? Should it treat them as *out-siders*, not children of God but 'children of wrath', not capable of any religious life pending the time when they will be old enough to be converted to God? From this it would follow that there can be no such thing as children's worship, and all we could do would be to teach children the facts and beliefs, as in a catechism, in the hope that they may begin to understand them later when they are old enough to be converted. We should not even on this view teach children to pray or to sing hymns. All these things would logically disappear if we are really to take the view that there is no such thing as the Christianity of childhood, and if the children of Christians are to pass through their early years not as Christian children but as little pagans, and outsiders, incapable of truly worshipping God. But surely very few, even of those who reject infant baptism, would adopt these conclusions. And in reply to any-one who did, it would be sufficient to use our Lord's shattering question: '*Have ye never read, Out of the mouth of babes and sucklings thou hast perfected praise?*'[1]

It is surely vital to realize that childhood is part of God's plan for human life, just as much as is manhood or womanhood. It

---

[1] Matthew xxi, 16.

is not His will that we should try to force upon little children an adult type of experience. It is His will that so long as they are children they should really be children, and if we do violence to that plan we may turn them into abnormal children who will grow up into the wrong kind of adults. But neither can it be His will that they should go through their childhood without any part or lot in Christ, for He Himself delighted in little children, and even said, 'Of such is the Kingdom of Heaven'. It is rather God's will that children should have such an experience of His grace and love as befits their stage of growth; in short, that they should be *Christian children*. Therefore they should be regarded as part of the Church of Christ, the entrance to which is marked by the sacrament of baptism. Cullmann and other scholars have indeed maintained, with fairly convincing arguments, that when the gospel tradition transmitted the story of Jesus blessing the children and telling the disciples not to forbid them, it did so with a definite view to a controversy about baptizing infants which had perhaps already begun.[1]

The first objection that will arise at this point is obvious. It will be asked; 'Even if children can have a genuine Christian faith, how far can that be extended back to their very early days, so as to cover infant baptism which is usually administered at an age when the recipient is incapable of receiving grace by *faith* and is even quite unconscious of what is being done?'

I would reply by suggesting that this objection is based upon a false individualism which is as far removed from the plain facts of life as it is from the Biblical outlook. A newborn child is the beginning of an immortal soul, but is not yet an independent soul. Decisions have to be made for him, by his parents and by the Church, and these cannot be postponed, because

---

[1] *Baptism in the New Testament*, English translation, pp. 25–26, and note, 42, 76ff. Cullman believes that the question τί κωλύει; (What hinders?) and the answer οὐδὲν κωλύει (Nothing hinders) were regularly used in the early Church before baptism was administered; as in Acts viii, 36. And he connects this with our Lord's words in Mark x, 13–14: μὴ κωλύετε αὐτα (Hinder them not).

life goes on and the child grows up in one way or another. So the Christian Church and Christian parents will choose the Christian life for their children. Does this mean that the benefits of the sacrament come to the child in response to the faith of the parents and of the Church? Yes, indeed; that is just what it means. They claim God's promise for the child, by faith. And that is just as it ought to be, and is in keeping with the whole outlook of the New Testament, which has none of our false individualism.

It is true of course, that most cases of baptism mentioned in the New Testament are cases of adults. That was inevitable in the early years of the Christian mission, and the same thing happens still in the early years of any new mission field, when most of the Christians are 'first generation' Christians who have come into the Church from outside as adults. But it would be thoroughly in keeping with the whole thought-world of the New Testament that when a man becomes a Christian, his whole household, as well as himself, should be baptized. To become a Christian meant entering into the redeemed community of the Church of Christ, the new Israel. As the initiation of a Gentile into the old religion was by circumcision and proselyte baptism, so the initiation into the new Israel was by Christian baptism.[1] And the new Israel did not ignore the family any more than did the old. Thus to a Jew it would seem the most natural thing in the world that when a man became a Christian, he should have his children baptized as well as himself, just as he had had his sons circumcised in their infancy and just as any proselyte coming into the Jewish community from outside should have his infant sons circumcised and baptized with proselyte baptism as well as himself.

Cullmann[2] has indeed shown that it is doubtful whether in the New Testament times children born to parents who were

---

[1] In the Patristic Age circumcision was regarded as having foreshadowed baptism as the 'seal' of God's people. Lampe quotes Barnabas, Justin, Odes of Solomon, Lactantius, Augustine, Aphraates. (*The Seal of the Spirit*, p. 84f.)

[2] Op. cit., pp. 62–70.

themselves already baptized Christians would be baptized *at all*, seeing that they were born within the covenant. Thus while it cannot be categorically said that any of the cases of baptism recorded in the New Testament included baptisms of infants[1], two things may be said with some confidence as a result of recent study of the thought-world of the New Testament in this respect.

First, it seems very unlikely that in New Testament times adult baptism was ever administered to persons who had been born of Christian parents; either they were baptized in infancy or it was considered unnecessary for them to be baptized at all.

And second, it seems highly likely that whether infants born of Christian parents were baptized at all or not, Christian baptism was administered *without delay* to the children of persons who by baptism came into the Christian Church from paganism. Thus it is not infant baptism, but the postponement to adult life of the baptism of those who are born of Christian parents, that seems to be inconsistent with New Testament thought. And even if it should be true that in the earliest times it was not considered necessary to baptize those born within the Christian community, since they were 'holy' by birth, yet, as recent scholarship has pointed out, that could not be the last word in primitive Christianity, because Christian baptism was regarded as fulfilment not only of Jewish proselyte baptism but also of circumcision; and thus there would naturally develop the practice of baptizing the infants born to Christians.[2]

It is interesting to note how very close to all this is the statement of the matter in the *Directory of Public Worship* drawn up by the Westminster Assembly in 1647. Far removed from all false individualism, that Directory teaches 'that the promise is made to believers and their seed; and that the seed and posterity of the faithful, born within the Church, have by their birth interest in the covenant, and right to the seal of it, and to the outward privileges of the Church . . .: that children by baptism

---

[1] For cases in which infants may be included see Acts xvi, 15, 33; xviii, 8, I Cor. i, 16.

[2] See Cullmann, op. cit., pp. 64 *et seq.*

are solemnly received into the bosom of the visible Church, distinguished from the world, and them that are without, and united with believers . . .: that they are Christians, and federally holy before baptism, and therefore are they baptized.'[1]

At this point the objector will come forward with what superficially may seem to be the most formidable objection of all. What difference does it make to a new-born child when he is baptized? If baptism were a 'bare sign', symbolizing the fact that children of believers have a place in the Church, or a mere service of dedication, this question would not arise. But if baptism is a sacrament, a means of grace, in which the recipient receives in faith the benefits of the Gospel, and thus has his faith strengthened, then the question inevitably rises whether this can in any sense be true of an infant who is incapable of exercising faith and who is unconscious of the whole proceeding. Therefore what difference can it make to the child?

I would begin my answer by pointing out that the *sacrament of baptism brings the child into a new environment*, the environment of the Church of Christ, which Calvin, following Cyprian, called the Mother of all who have God as their Father. In that sense the baptism even of an infant is, as the Westminster Confession puts it, 'an engrafting into Christ', who lives in the Church which is His Body; and the child is thenceforth surrounded by the life of the Church, an environment which touches him most closely in the life of his parents.

The objector may protest that the child might, for all practical purposes, have the same environment of the Church and the Christian home even if there were no sacrament of baptism at all. But that is not true. Of course God is not bound by His sacraments, and He may in His grace use any environment. But if all that I have been arguing is true, there must be a real and important difference between the environment given to a child by a Church which takes infant baptism seriously and the environment given by a Church which denies this sacrament to infants. A Church which practises infant baptism with real belief and understanding inevitably has an attitude to its

---

[1] Cf. I Cor. vii, 14.

children which makes it in a peculiar sense a means of grace to them; and every time the sacrament is administered to an infant 'in the face of the congregation' the Church and especially the parents are brought afresh into that attitude. In such a Church a child is indeed brought through baptism into a new and supernatural environment.

But what difference does that make at the time, or for long afterwards, to the child who is quite incapable of anything we could call 'the faith of the recipient'? In facing that question we must ask: When *does* the child become capable of the beginning of faith? If there is such a thing as a Christian child, a child's religion, at what age does this possibility begin? How far back can we go? And where shall we draw the line?

The answer is that we dare not draw the line at all. We do know that from the child's very earliest days, even in the pre-natal period, the environment matters immensely in determining his future development. And not merely his physical environment in the narrow sense, but his spiritual environment —the nervous, and therefore the mental and spiritual condition of the mother—,determining from the start whether the child is moulded along the lines of stress and strain, fear and disharmony and fretful ill-temper, or along the lines of harmony, trustfulness, good temper, faith and love.

And such truly Christian environment, working upon the child through physical media, tends to produce the latter mentality, and is thus from the very beginning a channel of God's grace to the child—a beginning for which we cannot draw the line anywhere at all.

Some years ago I heard a woman lecturer on child psychology say something which immediately seemed to me to have a bearing on sacramental doctrine. She was speaking of a hospital for motherless babies in India, and how, for lack of a mother, many of the babies pined away and died, however well-fed and attended. The nurses, of course, kept the usual rule of not handling the babies unnecessarily, but letting them lie in their cots with a regular routine and the minimum of interference. But one day, she told us, an Indian woman walking about the ward and dandling a baby in her arms said, 'Why don't you let the nurses dandle the babies? *A baby must have love*'. The lecturer went on to explain how nothing can take the place of that physical way of communicating affection, the maternal touch, the actual loving contact of the mother's or the foster-mother's hand with the baby's body—'epidermis against epidermis', and not for any purely physical reasons, but because 'a baby must have love', and only through that subconscious channel can the maternal love reach a child who has not yet any self-conscious existence at all.

When I heard the lecturer, I thought at once of the sacrament of baptism. If 'a baby must have love', it is also true that a baby must have the grace of God in order that it may grow as a truly Christian child. And it is through the faith and love of the Church and the parents, directed upon the child through physical channels, and using the effective symbolism of baptism, that the grace of God reaches the scarcely conscious child. And the half-unconscious trustfulness engendered in the child through this supernatural environment—is it not the beginning of the child's faith?

> *The Baby has no skies*
> *But Mother's eyes,*
> *Nor any God above*
> *But Mother's love.*
> *His angel sees the Father's face,*
> *But* he *the Mother's, full of grace;*
> *And yet the heavenly kingdom is*
> *Of such as this.'*[1]

This is no sentimentalism, nor is it magic, but sacramental doctrine. Let us remember what the austere Calvin said about the purpose of the sacraments; that God in His wonderful providence has accommodated Himself to our capacity, because in this mortal life we are not purely spiritual beings like the angels, but live in bodies of flesh.[2] And to those who asked how infants without any knowledge of good or evil could be re-

---

[1] Father John Banister Tabb.   [2] *Institutes*, Book IV, i, 1.

generated, or how faith, which 'cometh by hearing', could come to infants incapable of hearing the Word, Calvin replied that we must not limit the power of God, who works in ways we cannot perceive or understand, and who, to those incapable of hearing the Word, can give His grace otherwise.[1] Perhaps modern psychology has given us a clue beyond what Calvin could possess.

But the argument is not yet complete. There is something yet to be added for the full justification of infant baptism—something of very great importance. I may introduce it by quoting the following words from the Westminster Confession: 'The efficacy of baptism is not tied to that moment of time wherein it is administered; yet notwithstanding, by the right use of this ordinance, the grace promised is not only offered, but really exhibited and conferred by the Holy Ghost, to such (whether of age or infants) as that grace belongeth unto, according to the counsel of God's own will, in his appointed time.'[2] The latter part of the sentence covers what I have just been saying. But the first clause gives us something which I have not yet used in my argument. The point is that a person's baptism should be to him a means of grace, not merely at that moment but ever afterwards; and the faith which appropriates the grace offered in that sacrament includes the faith by which all his life long he looks back to his baptism.

So when the objectors asks, 'How can an unconscious child have faith? and therefore why should he be baptized?' I reply 'Why do you assume that the faith must come first, or simultaneously? Are you forgetting that, just because a person is baptized only once, the faith which afterwards looks back to it is part of its very meaning?' That is entirely in line with our whole conception of what a sacrament is. A sacrament is a sacred sign which faith uses for its strengthening and growth. Or better: a sacrament is a sacred sign which God uses for the quickening of our faith. And in the case of baptism the *sign* is given only once in the life of the individual, but its *efficacy* continues working through faith as we look back. So Calvin main-

[1] *Institutes*, Book IV, xvi, 17–19.   [2] Chapter xxviii, 6.

tains that infants are baptized into *future* repentance and faith, the seeds of which are implanted in their hearts by the Holy Spirit; and that according to New Testament teaching 'the thing signified' need not precede the sign, but may come after.

All this is, of course, in line with the principle laid down in the Westminster Directory of Public Worship that the adult Christian should look back to his baptism with understanding, and by faith use it as a means of grace.

It is deeply interesting to find in our own time Oscar Cullmann, as a New Testament scholar, on the basis of a careful examination of the conception of baptism present in the New Testament, coming to a conclusion which thoroughly bears out this position. According to the New Testament, on Cullmann's exposition, the background and presupposition of this sacrament is the general baptism for *all* men accomplished on Calvary.[1] What happens in the actual administration of the sacrament is that the individual baptized is thereby set by God within the Body of Christ. In the case of an adult coming over from Judaism or paganism a declaration of personal faith is demanded of the praying congregation *during* baptism; but also faith is demanded *after* baptism of all who are baptized, and thus the efficacy extends through the whole subsequent life of the person baptized.

In that sense our faith is a response to what God does for us first on Calvary and then in our baptism. *God's initiative precedes our faith; our faith follows.* Surely it is in *subsequent* faith going on right through a man's life that, above all, the sacrament becomes efficacious and a channel of the grace of God.

It is well known that Luther, throughout his life, when oppressed by the sense of sin and judgement, used to say to himself, for the encouragement of his faith: '*Baptizatus sum*, I was baptized.' And so, as Cullmann says 'the complete baptismal event' extends through the whole life.

This raises the question so much debated in recent years of

[1] For an elaborate working out of this, see J. A. T. Robinson's article 'The One Baptism' in *Scottish Journal of Theolgy*, September 1953, pp. 257–274.

the relation between baptism and confirmation in the complete process of Christian initiation. Into that large question I cannot now enter. *But* if we of the Reformed tradition do defend infant baptism on the lines I have indicated (as I believe we must), then surely it follows that we must make much more than we have often done of the subsequent step, whether we call it confirmation or anything else, when the baptized person, having come to years of understanding, makes profession of faith and is admitted to full communion. For whatever else the individual does at that point, he ought to be laying hold by faith of what was given him as an infant in the sacrament of baptism.[1]

---

[1] *Confirmation.* The word seems to occur first in the fifth century—in 441, and again in a letter of Pope Leo I in 458. Did it mark a change of emphasis in the rite of initiation? See Dix, *The Theology of Confirmation*, p. 21. This lecture illustrates the endless confusion and disagreement from early centuries through the Middle Ages down to modern times as to whether confirmation was a sacrament at all and its relation to baptism and its *meaning* (who or what was confirmed). For the idea that confirmation was a 'strengthening' of the graces given in the baptism, or of the confirmed, see ibid. p. 26ff.

The Reformed (Calvinistic) view of baptism makes room excellently for a doctrine of confirmation, whether it is a sacrament or not; and *not* in a sense which detracts from baptism, but in a sense based on the extension of the effect of baptism through the whole of life.

LECTURE IV

The Real Presence

❦

When I look back to my childhood and boyhood in the Highlands of Scotland (as I ventured for a moment to do in my first lecture) I can never forget that in those days and in that environment the sacrament of the Lord's supper meant a very great deal in the life of a faithful community. It was surrounded by an atmosphere of mystery and awe and holy reverence. The emphasis on its solemnity was indeed so extreme and one-sided that only a small minority of the regular church-goers, in Highland Presbyterianism, ever took the step of becoming communicants at all: the rest of the people, while faithfully attending public worship, and even the communion service, considered themselves unworthy to sit at the Lord's table and to receive the sacred symbols of His body and blood, 'lest they should eat and drink judgement on themselves'. Moreover every celebration of the Lord's supper was preceded by several days of preparatory services, beginning on the Thursday, which was treated as a fast, and going through the Friday and Saturday, so that the actual communion service on the Sunday morning was the climax of what was called a 'communion season'; and it was followed by services of thanksgiving on the Sunday evening and even on the Monday morning. All this was possible of course because communion was celebrated in any one parish only once or twice a year. That infrequency may seem strangely out of accord with the high value placed upon the sacrament, and with the principles of our forefathers at the Westminster Assembly who declared that celebration should be frequent. But in those days in the Scottish Highlands it was not uncommon for the most ardent spirits to secure greater frequency of communion for themselves by attending the 'communion seasons' of other parishes up to a considerable distance. I am not contending that all was well in this conception and practice of communion (far from it!). But at least it was a real sacrament, holy, supernatural, sanctifying, a great and potent means of grace to the most devout members of the Church.

I cannot close my eyes to the fact that to most people in the tradition to which I belong the sacrament means less now. Is that true of all the Protestant Churches? Have they all lost something of its meaning and power? Or may we venture to hope that after a period of loss we are recapturing some of it now? I believe that is beginning to happen in Scotland. And it has happened even more in certain Anglican or Episcopalian quarters. No doubt some Anglo-Catholics are mere pseudo-sacramentalists without any real understanding of the deep things of Christian worship (as many of their fellow churchmen would be the first to acknowledge). But there are many others whose sacramental approach is profoundly Christian and to whom Holy Communion means everything. I once heard a highly intellectual and deeply devout and Christian Anglo-Catholic say: 'To me Christianity simply *means*—the blessed sacrament.' I once heard a young woman student, again a deeply Christian Anglo-Catholic, say that she simply *lived* on her weekly Communion and could not get on without it.

Could many of us Presbyterians say that kind of thing about this sacrament which from the very beginning in the New Testament was the central service of the Christian Church? And if not, why not? Can we be quite content with the situation? It is of course true that our tradition has always refused to make the sacraments more central than the Word. But it has always in its great days refused to separate the Word and the sacraments from each other. And if the sacrament means less to us than it did to our forefathers, is it because the Word means more to us? I am afraid that it is not. Doubtless we should all wish to criticise the Anglo-Catholic doctrine of the eucharist on such matters as the Real Presence and the eucharistic sacrifice. But if we cannot get beyond a merely negative criticism, we may, when asked for our doctrine of the Lord's supper, be found offering a stone instead of bread. Surely if we reject their doctrines, it is not because *they believe too much.* Surely we are not going to be content with believing *less* than they do—content with a smaller, poorer belief. Surely if we criticize Roman or Anglo-Catholic eucharistic doctrine, it will be because we claim that we have some better and richer and higher belief about what God gives us in the sacrament.

But I am not mainly concerned to criticize the doctrines of those other traditions, or to make a gulf between them and our own views: I would be much better pleased if it emerged from my discussion that they and we are nearer to each other than we sometimes think. It would be quite impossible in these last two lectures of the course to discuss the many complex historical questions about the origins of the eucharist, or even to make a full study of the eucharistic doctrine that we find in various parts of the New Testament. Really our doctrine of the eucharist must be based not on such passages alone, but on the whole of the New Testament conception of Christianity.

Let us begin by thinking of:

THE DRAMATIC SYMBOLISM OF THE LORD'S SUPPER

Every school of theological thought, and every Church, speaks of this sacrament as a 'sensible sign' or a symbol. That is of the very essence of a sacrament. This is not to say that the sacraments are *merely* signs or symbols. They are more. But if they were not signs, they could not be more. It is through being signs, through their symbolism, that they come to be more. And that seems to me to be of particular importance for our Reformed theology of the eucharist.

But further: not only is the eucharist a piece of symbolism, it is a piece of *dramatic* symbolism. In order to make quite plain what I mean by that, let me remind you of the important fact, often forgotten, that the 'sensible signs' in this sacrament consist not only of the elements, the bread and the wine, but also of *the actions*, including the words spoken; but neither the words nor the elements as apart from the actions. P. T. Forsyth maintained that in the original 'Last Supper' it was not so much the bread as the breaking, not so much the elements as the actions, that were symbolical.[1] Dom Gregory Dix says that while the modern Anglican thinks of the eucharist as something *said*, the New Testament and the early Church thought of it as something *done*.[2] Thus the eucharist consists of a complex pattern of elements, words and actions, a pattern which has a symbolical meaning. That is why it is sometimes called an 'acted parable'; and some writers have found a background to the Christian sacraments not so much in the ceremonies of the Hebrew temple worship as in those dramatic acted parables which some of the Hebrew prophets (notably Ezekiel) sometimes employed as an expression of their message. Thus we seem to be justified in saying that the eucharist follows a method of dramatic representation or symbolism.

Let us try to see in what sense this is a justifiable approach to the interpretation of the eucharist. It is worth noting, and perhaps a little surprising, that Roman Catholic divines seem more disposed than Protestants to use this approach. Doubtless that is partly because the Roman celebration has so much more ritual and colour than our own celebration—it may literally be called a more 'dramatic' performance. One might expect the *ex opere operato* doctrine of the Roman Church to make the dramatic aspect of the eucharist less important, and any strong emphasis upon it less desirable. But that is not what we find. Abbot Herwegen, of the Benedictine monastery of Maria Laach, who was the leader of a really wholesome liturgical movement in Roman Catholic Germany, wrote a booklet

[1] *The Church and the Sacraments* (1917), Fourth impression (1953) p. 234ff.
[2] *The Shape of the Liturgy* (1945), p. 12.

called *The Artistic Principle of the Liturgy*,[1] in which he offered a kind of running commentary on the mass as a work of art which, as it moves on from one phase to another, sets before the worshipper in dramatic form the great truths and realities of the Christian faith. The same thing is done in a different way by Monsignor Ronald Knox in his book *The Mass In Slow Motion*, the very title of which indicates the nature of the treatment. The mass is taken as a spectacle, as it were on the screen, but slowed down for purposes of exposition, so that the commentator can explain the meaning of each successive phase of the action of the drama. And as another example, here is a remarkable passage by the Roman Catholic theologian Eugene Masure: 'It is certain that the Mass, considered as a work of ritual art, is a pure masterpiece of tranquil beauty. Colour, sound, movement, all the aesthetic resources of the human body in its symbolic actions, are united and bound together in a context of splendid, stylised archaism around this altar barely lit with a few candles to produce one of the wonders of religious history. But behind all this beauty there is a hidden drama, whose spring and movement we must penetrate—but not the eternal and invisible drama, the Passion of Christ which is here renewed or His heavenly sacrifice which is here communicated. . . . What we are speaking of is the movement of the liturgy itself, of the divine plot which is developed and resolved throughout this spectacle, the ceremony's hidden soul, the secret of all this anxiety, the inner explanation of it.' And then the writer goes on through several pages to trace the stages of this drama, from the preparation of the priest at the foot of the altar steps to the final 'grand gesture of farewell and benediction'.[2]

Now we of the Reformed tradition may very naturally find that approach somewhat uncongenial, even though the symbolic aspect of the eucharist is so very important for us. It may even seem to us that the element of very elaborate and imaginative drama, with so much emphasis on aesthetic considerations, is alien to our conception of the sacrament. Dr. H. J.

[1] *Das Kunstprinzip der Liturgie*, 2nd Edition, 1920.
[2] *The Christian Sacrifice*. 1944, English translation, p. 250ff.

Wotherspoon, who wrote the best book Scotland has produced on the sacraments for a long time, says that a sacrament 'speaks not to the imagination, but to faith, and the faith to which it speaks is faith in God, that He is true to His own appointment'.[1] Professor Karl Barth has a remarkable passage about the genius and failure of the Roman mass. 'The mass in its conception, content and construction is a religious masterpiece. It is the highwater mark in the development of the history of religion and admits of no rival.' But then he goes on to say that that is just what is wrong with it. 'Religion with its masterpieces is one thing, Christian faith is another.'[2] What Barth means is that the sacrament must be regarded not as something thought out by the Church from the point of view of solemnity, beauty, drama, education, psychology, mystery, and so on, but as a matter of obedience to Christ and complete faithfulness to His gospel. Yes, of course; the sacrament of the Lord's supper has its essential and inseparable connection with Jesus Christ, and the one question about any eucharistic liturgy is where and how far it expresses and represents the truths and realities of His Gospel. But *if* the Roman liturgy fails to do these things, then surely it is *not* a religious masterpiece from the Christian point of view, and what is wrong with it is not its use of dramatic symbolism which in some sense every sacrament must use, but that it makes, to some extent, the wrong use of it and symbolizes the wrong things.

That is really the question that we have to ask about the sacrament of the Lord's supper: what are the realities that it ought to symbolize if it is to be true to the Gospel of Christ? As a sacrament it uses 'sensible signs'. Signs of what? What are the things signified? In answering that question we must discuss two elements of meaning that have traditionally been found in this sacrament: the Real Presence and the eucharistic sacrifice.

The second of these we shall discuss in the fifth and last lecture. To the first of them, the Real Presence, we will now turn.

---

[1] *Religious Values in the Sacraments*, 1928, p. 21.
[2] *The Knowledge of God and the Service of God*, p. 206f.

THE REAL PRESENCE

In what sense does our Reformed theology teach the Real Presence in the sacrament of the Lord's supper? There is no doubt that traditionally it has taught that not only the *signum*, the sign, is present, but also the *res*, the thing signified; that is, it has believed in the *praesentia realis*. The Westminster Confession of Faith says: 'Worthy receivers, outwardly partaking of the visible elements in this sacrament, do then also inwardly by faith, really and indeed, yet not carnally and corporally, but spiritually, receive and feed upon Christ crucified, and all the benefits of His death: the body and blood of Christ being then not corporally or carnally in, with, or under the bread and wine; yet as really, but spiritually, present to the faith of believers in that ordinance, as the elements themselves are to their outward senses.'[1] What does that mean? Is that a subjective or an objective presence? Of course it is objective. To say it is merely subjective would mean that we *imagine* Christ to be there though He is not really there. To say 'subjective' would be to deny that very objectivity and prevenience of the divine of which it is the very function of the sacraments to remind us.

It is sometimes asked: 'Do we Protestants take a *realistic* view of the divine presence in the sacraments?' Surely the answer is 'Yes'. Surely we cannot be content to say that Roman Catholics or Anglo-Catholics make the divine presence in the sacrament *more real* than we do. But what do we mean by Real Presence? Is it different in the sacrament from the kind of divine presence we can have at any time when we draw near to God?

It is important to note that even apart from the sacrament we are bound to distinguish several degrees or modes of the divine presence. To begin with the most general, we believe in the *omnipresence* of God. He is everywhere present. And yet we also say that God is with those who trust and obey Him in a way in which He is not with others. We say, God is with them.

[1] Chapter XXIX, vii.

And we say that God's presence is with us *more* at some times than at others. We speak of entering into His presence in worship, and we ask Him to come and be with us and grant us His presence. We say that wherever two or three are gathered together in His name, He is there in the midst of them. And then in apparently a still further sense we speak of the Real Presence in the sacrament. What does all that mean?

Surely the first thing we have to remember is that God's presence is not strictly speaking a *local* or *spatial* presence at all, but a spiritual personal relationship which we have to symbolise by spatial metaphors. When we say that God is everywhere present, that does not mean that He fills every portion of space. For God is not in space at all. Space is part of His creation, and He Himself transcends it. And His omnipresence, as a Christian doctrine, means that wherever we are in this world of space and time, we are not away from God, and He is not absent. What then of His special presence with certain people on certain occasions? Surely that is a spiritual relationship, not less real on that account: we might even say *more real*, because this presence is something much greater, more besetting, more penetrating than any merely local or spatial presence could be. But there are degrees in this relationship. God has a certain spiritual relation to His whole creation, even the material world, in the sense that its very existence and functioning from moment to moment depend upon His will. There is a further degree of this presence in the relationship between God and man, because now there is the beginning of a personal relationship, in the sense that it is only through being *addressed* by God that man is man at all as a personal responsible being. There is a still further stage when man responds to that divine address by personal faith and obedience; so that God is specially present to the faith of the believer or, better still, to the faith of a fellowship of believers in worship, where two or three are gathered together in His name.

There are some profound pages in Gabriel Marcel's Gifford Lectures about the true meaning of the preposition 'with'. He points out that 'with' properly indicates an 'intersubjective relationship', a spiritual relationship between persons, and not a mere juxtaposition in space. Thus it does not apply at all to a world of objects. A chair may be *alongside* a table, and *beside* a table, but not really *with* the table in the true sense. And there may even be two persons together in a room without their being in more than a minimal way *with* each other, because they are not encountering each other in a genuine relationship.[1] So 'We can . . . have a very strong feeling that somebody who is sitting in the same room as ourselves, sitting quite near us, someone whom we can look at and listen to and whom we could touch if we wanted to make a final test of his reality, is nevertheless more distant from us than some loved one who is perhaps thousands of miles away or perhaps, even, no longer among the living. We could say that the man sitting beside us was in the same room as ourselves, but that he was not really *present* there, that his *presence* did not make itself felt.'[2] Marcel is not thinking at all of sacramental doctrine, but these thoughts seem to me to be most relevant to the question of the real presence in the sacrament.

All this reaches its climax in the sacrament of the Lord's supper, where the God who was incarnate in Jesus uses the symbolism of the sacrament as a special means of awakening the faith of His people that they may receive Him, since faith is the channel by which God's most intimate presence comes to men in this earthly life.

It is indeed true that both Lutheran and Reformed theology have sometimes taken crude and unsatisfying ways of defining that Real Presence. That is especially true of John Calvin himself. He speaks in the most literal way of the flesh of Christ being present in the sacrament. He has to reconcile this with the body of Christ being actually in heaven, at an immense distance from the earth, and to him it is simply a mystery and a miracle that through the supernatural power of God this distance is bridged and the flesh of Christ is present. Of course

[1] *Reflection and Mystery*, 1950, p. 177.
[2] *Ibid.*, p. 205.

99

he does not teach that the body and blood of Christ are locally present *in the elements*; yet they are spiritually present—not merely believed or imagined to be present, but truly and really present to the faith of the believer. Obviously Calvin is trying very hard to secure the utmost objectivity and reality for the presence of Christ in the sacrament, and at the same time to avoid all the magical, mechanical and spatial implications of saying that the body and blood of Christ are *in* the bread and the wine, or that there is a change in the elements such as is defined by the Roman doctrine of transubstantiation.

But it seems very important to realize that the doctrine of transubstantiation itself was an attempt, however unsuccessful and unsound, to avoid crude and materialistic conceptions of what happens in the sacrament, and even to save the idea of the Real Presence from a crudely spatial interpretation. I owe my understanding of this to Canon Lilley's admirable little book entitled *Sacraments*. When the medieval divines, and finally St. Thomas Aquinas, worked out the doctrine of transubstantiation, they were doubtless assuming an Aristotelian metaphysic of substance and attributes which we can no longer accept, but they were endeavouring to spiritualize a conception of the miracle of the altar which was already dominant in the minds of the people, and the result was far less 'materialistic' than we commonly suppose. When the Roman doctrine teaches that in the miracle of the altar the substance of the bread and wine is changed into the substance of the body and blood of Christ, while the 'accidents', the sensible qualities, remain unchanged, this does not mean that the body of Christ is locally or spatially contained *in* the bread, as it were inside it, so that if you peeled off the surface you would find the flesh of Christ. After all, according to the scholastic metaphysic, the spatial properties belong to the accidents, not to the substance. The substance (whether of the elements or of the body) is not, strictly speaking, in space at all. And therefore the Real Presence is not, strictly speaking, a *local* presence *in* the elements—even on the transubstantialist view. Surely what the Roman doctrine at its best is struggling (with a very inadequate metaphysic) to conceive is the reality and objectivity of the divine presence as something prevenient and given, if only we will accept it.[1]

And surely it is the same truth that we Presbyterians are endeavouring to express in a safer and surer way when we say that in the sacrament Christ is as truly present to the faith of the receiver as the bread and wine are to his outward senses. 'Present to the faith of the receiver'—that is the most real presence conceivable for a divine reality in this present world. The most objective and penetrating kind of presence that God can give us is *through faith*. Any other kind of presence, any local or spatial divine presence, if we could conceive it, would be less real, less besetting, less intimate. St. Paul's prayer for his friends at Ephesus is 'that Christ may dwell in your hearts through faith'.[2] That is how Christ dwells in men's hearts in this present world.

This does not mean that somehow we conjure up the divine presence by believing in it, or that we produce the faith out of our own resources and that in response to our faith God gives us His presence. Nay, God is prevenient, and faith depends on His actions; He calls it forth, and that is His way of coming to dwell in a man or a company of men. That is what He does when He uses the symbolism of the bread and the wine, the words and the actions, to give Himself to us in the sacrament of the Lord's supper.

Sometimes the question is asked (by people who are more 'evangelical' than 'sacramentalist'): Are we saved by faith or by sacraments? Surely that is a false antithesis and alternative. The truth is that we are saved by neither, but by God. But He saves us through faith, and therefore partly through sacraments, which He uses to awaken and to strengthen our faith. Thus the sacrament of the Lord's supper is indeed a means of

[1] Dom Gregory Dix says that the preoccupation of Western theology with the metaphysical problem of the relation of the elements to the body of Christ was a result of the medieval emphasis on *seeing* the action of the eucharist, since it could not be *heard* in the vernacular, as the words were in Latin. (*The Shape of the Liturgy*, p. 621.) No wonder then, that the Reformers insisted that the sacraments must never be separated from the Word!

[2] Ephesians iii, 17.

grace, an instrument of salvation. And how can the Reformed Churches ever recover the meaning and potency of the sacrament until they approach it in that way? The danger is that in endeavouring to restore the power of the sacrament, we should strain ourselves to work up effects, to produce in ourselves devout and salutary effects, and thus in celebrating it to concentrate on ourselves, our own feelings, our own emotions, our own psychological states; which is the very opposite of what a sacrament should mean. The sacrament, by giving us not only words, but visible and tangible elements, should draw our thoughts away from ourselves to that great divine reality which is even nearer and more truly real than the things we can see with our eyes and touch with our hands. The Lord's supper is indeed the sacrament of the Real Presence.

But this leads us to a further stage of the argument which may be summed up under the following heading.

THE PRESENCE, THE MEMORY AND THE HOPE

A moment ago, in speaking of *faith* as the mode of the divine presence with us, I used repeatedly the phrase, 'in this present world'. We must now return to that phrase, because it reminds us of a situation which, as we saw in the second lecture, is of the very meaning of the sacraments. While the Lord's supper is indeed the sacrament of the Real Presence, it belongs also to a situation in which we are not in the 'immediate presence of God', and indeed to a situation in which we stand between a memory and a hope, looking backward to the incarnation and forward to the final consummation. We saw that the theology of our time has in various quarters come to a new understanding of the nature of the Church as belonging to that interim period; and that is immensely important for the sacrament of the Lord's supper. For the Real Presence in the sacrament is in a paradoxical sense a presence-in-absence. There is a sense in which, as St. Paul puts it, 'we are absent from the Lord'.[1] His presence with us is not of the same mode as it was with His

[1] II Cor., v, 6.

disciples in the days of His flesh, nor of the same mode as it will be when we come to see 'face to face'.[1] Thus it is of the very nature of this sacrament that it points back to the one and forward to the other.

On the one hand it is *a memorial feast*. None of the great Churches has ever reduced it to this alone, but each has always regarded this as part of its meaning. The Lord's supper must always be, among other things, in remembrance of Jesus Christ and particularly of His passion, and all its other meanings must depend on that historical reference; for it is an historical reference—the Church's corporate memory of the episode of the cross of Christ. Archbishop Brilioth remarks that the historical reference of the eucharist, as commemoration of an actual event, sharply distinguishes it from all such celebrations in the Greek mysteries where the historical actuality of the cult-story does not matter at all. It does matter vitally for Christianity, and the historical reference to the passion of Christ controls the whole meaning of the eucharist. St. Paul says, 'As often as you eat this bread and drink this cup, you do show the Lord's death until He come.'[2] He may have meant that the action of taking and breaking the bread and pouring out the wine is a dramatic representation of the death of Christ, who, as he says elsewhere, had been publicly portrayed or placarded, as crucified, before the eyes of the Galatians.[3] But some scholars think the Greek word translated 'ye do show' or 'portray' ought to be given its more natural sense and translated 'You do announce' or 'proclaim' or even 'recite'. Thus the sentence may mean: 'whenever you celebrate the Lord's supper, you recite the story of the passion'. If so, it would indicate that in St. Paul's time it was the custom to recite that whole story at the Lord's table, and this might well account for the fact that the part of the Gospel story which narrates the final scenes is out of all proportion fuller and more detailed than all the rest of the story; all the details were faithfully preserved because from the earliest days they were being continually recited in the weekly worship of the Church.

[1] I Cor., xiii, 12.   [2] I Cor., xi, 26.   [3] Gal., iii, 1.

In any case that must always be a determinative part of the meaning of this sacrament. We do this because of what Jesus did with His disciples in the upper room in Jerusalem on the night before His crucifixion and we 'do this in remembrance' of Him, and particularly of His death. Christianity can never get away from the Jesus of history, and so the Church's corporate memory of Him must always be a vital part of its central act of worship, the Lord's supper.

But in this sacrament the Church has not only a present enjoyment and a memory of the past, it also has a looking forward into the future.

The words to which I have just referred, 'This do in remembrance (*anamnēsin*) of me' have been much discussed in recent years, and various scholars have suggested that they mean much more than a memory of the past, and that indeed the usual translation is a quite inadequate rendering of the Greek words. I shall have to return to this in the next lecture when I come to discuss the eucharistic sacrifice. But at this point I must refer to an interpretation of the words which has been offered by Professor Jeremias of Göttingen, who has made a special study of all the words used by Jesus in the story of the Last supper. He suggests that the words referred to have a kind of eschatological reference; that the 'remembrance' is not merely a human memory of the past but a memorial before God, in somewhat the same sense in which, in the Acts of the Apostles, the angel says to Cornelius, 'your prayers and your alms have ascended as a memorial before God'.[1] (But in this verse the Greek word is not *anamnēsis* but *mnēmosunon*.) Thus the words would mean: 'Do this as a reminder to God on my behalf, that God may have me, His Messiah, in remembrance, to bring about my *parousia* with the Kingdom.'[2] Whatever we may think of that exegesis, it seems clear that in its origins the sacrament had that future reference. Various scholars have emphasized this. Professor Macgregor maintains that for St. Paul's conception of the eucharist the remembrance of the

[1] Acts x, 4.
[2] *Journal of Theological Studies*, Vol. L, 1949, p. 9.

dying and returning of Christ is primary.[1] Dom Gregory Dix says that in early Christianity 'the whole conception of *anamnēsis* is in itself eschatological. . . . What the Church "remembers" in the eucharist is partly *beyond* history—the ascension, the sitting at the right hand of the Father and the second coming.'[2] (Dix goes on to say that in the fourth century the *anamnēsis* came to include explicit mention of the ascension, the sitting at the right hand of the Father and the last judgment, though he thinks this somewhat distorted the primitive conception.) Oscar Cullmann maintains that the early Christian ejaculatory prayer (which was so early that it was actually handed down in its Aramaic form) *Marana tha*, 'Come Lord', had both an eschatological and a present sense. It meant at the same time 'Come and grant us now Thy presence in our worship' and 'Come in power and glory', so that the note of the Real Presence and the note of eschatology were blended in one.

Here also is a remarkable and often quoted passage from C. H. Dodd, which has deep truth even for those who cannot accept his entire theory of 'realized' eschatology. 'In the Eucharist, therefore, the Church perpetually reconstitutes the crisis in which the Kingdom of God came in history. It never gets beyond this. At each Eucharist we are *there*—we are in the night in which He was betrayed, at Golgotha, before the empty tomb on Easter Day, and in the upper room where He appeared; *and* we are at the moment of His coming, with angels and archangels and all the company of heaven, in the twinkling of an eye at the last trump. Sacramental communion is not a purely mystical experience, to which history, as embodied in the form and matter of the sacrament, would be in the last resort irrelevant; it is bound up with a corporate memory of real events.'[3] Edmund Schlink also writes, 'In the Lord's supper we already share here on earth in that future glory. In the Lord's supper we are present at the death of Christ and at His return, at His first and second advent.'[4]

[1] G. H. C. Macgregor, *Eucharistic Origins*, p. 173f.   [2] Op. cit., p. 263ff.
[3] *The Apostolic Preaching and Its Developments*, 1936, p. 234f.
[4] In *Intercommunion*, edited by Donald Baillie and John Marsh (1952), p. 296.

Such passages show magnificently how at this sacrament we have the presence, the memory and the hope all in one.

St. Paul is plainly conscious of standing between that past and the future, between the memory and the hope, when he tells the Corinthian Christians what the Lord's supper is. 'I received from the Lord what I handed on to you, that on the night of His betrayal the Lord Jesus took bread, and when He had given thanks, He brake it and said; Take, eat, this is my body which is broken for you; this do in remembrance of me. . . . As often as you eat this bread, and drink this cup, you proclaim the Lord's *death until He come*.'[1] The early Church was most vividly and intensely conscious of living in that interval every time it met for worship and celebrated the supper; most intensely conscious of it because to them the interval appeared as a very short one. The thing they remembered from the *past*— the death of Christ—was in the very recent past, and many had seen His Cross with their eyes. And the thing to which they looked forward in the future seemed to them to be in the very near future—they thought the Lord was going to return in their own lifetime. The Church and the sacrament were indeed eschatological realities to them.

To us, perhaps, it is far more difficult to make that aspect real; partly, perhaps, because in certain sectarian quarters the very idea of a second advent has been used in foolish and sensational ways, and partly because even in the most responsible theological quarters the very word 'eschatological' has been used too much in recent years, and used even as a piece of jargon.

But surely it is profoundly true (as we said in a previous lecture) that the reason why we need this sacrament at all is because in this present world we are strangers and pilgrims, and all human history is a pilgrimage towards something that lies beyond, some supernal reality, a Kingdom of God in which sacramental symbols will not any longer be needed because God Himself will be its temple.

I want to read you a passage from a letter written by that

[1] I Cor., xi, 23–26.

great Scottish churchman and theologian, Principal D. S. Cairns. After quoting Jesus' words at the last supper, 'Verily I say unto you, I will drink no more of the fruit of the vine until the day that I drink it new with you in the Kingdom of God', Cairns goes on, 'At the very nadir of defeat and solitude, He founds a rite and sends it down through all history, which will be a continual prophecy of victory. In the sacrament we are really rehearsing, or rather anticipating, the day when the whole human race will be home, gathered round the Father's table, after Iliads and Odysseys yet to be! Retrospect and prophecy is one; that is what the sacrament is to me, with renewal of the covenant face to face.'[1] That sums up the whole matter of the memory, the hope and the presence.

One final word. Baron Von Hügel never tired of telling of a thing that St. Bernard of Clairvaux used to say to his monks. He said to them that however early they might wake and rise for prayer in their chapel on a dark midwinter morning, or even in the dead of night, they would always find God awake before them, waiting for them—nay rather, it was God Himself who had wakened them to seek His face. It may be that in those distant Middle Ages devout men thought of God as literally waiting for them in the Host on the altar. We could not think of it like that. But surely to us His Presence should be just as real in our celebration of the sacrament.

And one result of our recovery of a deep and strong sacramental theology will be this: that we shall learn to approach the Lord's table not looking inwards upon our own souls and striving to work up an effect in the realm of feeling and emotion, but looking beyond ourselves to Him who is waiting to be gracious to us, Him who answers before we call and hears while we are yet speaking, Him who in His grace and love is as near and as real as the bread which we see with our eyes and touch with our hands.

---

[1] *David Cairns: An Autobiography*, 1950, p. 201.

LECTURE V

The Eucharistic Offering

❧

I
n recent years I have had a considerable share in discussions under the auspices of the World Council of Churches between churchmen of many traditions and from many countries on the subject of intercommunion.

In the course of these discussions I have become aware that *one* of the main obstacles to intercommunion between the Churches is the suspicion that different Churches mean different things by the sacrament of Holy Communion: some regard the sacrament as a *sacrifice* and to them that is quite essential and central, while others repudiate that interpretation altogether. I want to suggest that apart from the Church of Rome, which remains entirely outside the World Council of Churches, the difference between the Churches on the question of eucharistic sacrifice may not be so extreme as is often supposed.

It is important to realize at the very outset that the division of opinion does not quite coincide with any denominational boundaries but cuts across them. Most Anglo-Catholics (and these include many excellent theologians to-day) would lay immense emphasis on the doctrine of the eucharistic sacrifice,[1] and yet there are a great many members of the Anglican communion who would disagree with them strongly.

One of the Articles of the Church of England (XXXI),

[1] Cf. the articles and letters on this subject in the various issues of the journal *Theology* during 1953.

headed 'Of the one Oblation of Christ finished upon the Cross', says (in reference, of course, to the Roman Catholic mass): 'Wherefore the sacrifice of masses, in the which it was commonly said, that the priest did offer Christ for the quick and the dead, to have remission of pain or guilt, were blasphemous fables and dangerous deceits,' and many Anglicans would interpret that as a repudiation of the whole idea of eucharistic sacrifice. As for us Presbyterians, the Westminster Confession of 1647 teaches that 'In this sacrament Christ is not offered up to His Father, nor any real sacrifice made at all for remission of sins of the quick or dead'; and goes on to say (in a style reminiscent of the Anglican article) that 'The Popish sacrifice of the mass, as they call it, is most abominably injurious to Christ's one only sacrifice, the alone propitiation for all the sins of the elect.'[1]

It is quite plain that these expressions of strong repudiation, both in the Anglican article and the Westminster Confession, are due to a violent reaction against the abuses and superstitions connected with the Roman mass in the Middle Ages. But we must ask: 'Is there any truth at all in the idea that the sacrament of Holy Communion, properly and fully understood, contains something of the element of oblation, sacrifice or offering?' Quite apart from the Church of Rome, the Eastern Church has always made much of that element, and now there are many in the churches of the West who would claim to have rediscovered it. Certainly from the early years of the second century, if not earlier, Christian writers did speak of the eucharist as a sacrifice. Bishop Gore in his remarkable book, *The Body of Christ*, writes that 'There can be no doubt that from the earliest days the Christian Church thought of the eucharist as a sacrifice.'[2] The *Didache*, which may have been written before the end of the first century, and thus definitely within the New Testament period, contains the following passage: 'On every Lord's Day gather yourselves together and break bread and give thanks, first confessing your transgressions, that your

---

[1] Chap. XXIX, ii.   [2] p. 157.

sacrifice may be pure. And let no man, having his dispute with his fellows, join your assembly until they have been reconciled, that your sacrifice may not be defiled; for this sacrifice it is that was spoken of by the Lord, when he said, "In every place and at every time offer me a pure sacrifice; for I am a great king, saith the Lord, and my name is wonderful among the nations".[1] But can we say that there is in the New Testament itself any trace of the interpretation of the sacrament as a sacrifice?

At this point I must return to the consideration of that sentence on which I dwelt briefly in the last lecture: 'This do in remembrance of me.' The Greek text runs: *touto poieite eis tēn emēn anamnēsin*. A good deal has been written about these words in recent years, and sometimes with the contention that they mean much more than 'Do this in memory of me', and that they really have a sacrificial sense. Scholars have pointed out that in the Septuagint the Greek verb *poiein* can mean not only 'do', but also 'offer' or 'sacrifice' in translation of a Hebrew word which has both meanings. Time after time it is used in passages where the English has 'offer'. Thus in the account of the institution of the Lord's supper it might be argued that we ought to translate not 'do this' but 'make this sacrifice' or even 'offer this bread and this wine'. And as regards the words that follow, *eis tēn emēn anamnēsin*, it has been contended that these also can be translated in a way which carries on the sacrificial import. Dom Gregory Dix says that this word *anamnēsis* 'is not quite easy to represent accurately in English, words like "remembrance" or "memorial" having for us a connotation of something itself absent which is only mentally recollected. But in the Scriptures, both of the Old and the New Testament, *anamnēsis* and the cognate verb have the sense of "re-calling" or "representing" before God an event in the past so that it becomes here and now operative by its effects.' Along these lines it can be argued that the words usually translated 'do this in remembrance of me' really mean something like 'make this offering of the bread and the wine as a memorial before God of

---

[1] Chap. XIV.

the sacrifice of Christ, as a re-presentation to God of that sacrifice'. What are we to make of that interpretation?[1]

I am not primarily a New Testament scholar, and in this point of historical exegesis I am largely dependent on others. But I do not think that a directly sacrificial meaning can be safely read into the words. Fifty years ago Bishop Gore, himself an Anglo-Catholic, discussed the matter and came to a negative conclusion. He knew, of course, that in the Septuagint the word *poiein* regularly had the sense of 'sacrifice'. As regards *anamnēsis*, he knew that in the Septuagint it could mean much more than mere human remembrance, and he quotes Lev. xxiv. 7: the shew-bread 'shall be for a memorial (*anamnēsis*) lying before the Lord.'

But he goes on to point out that the word *anamnēsis* in the institution of the sacrament was apparently *not* understood in the early Church in the sense of a sacrificial memorial before God but rather in the sense of a human remembrance. It may indeed be true that the familiar translation 'This do in remembrance of me' does not exhaust the meaning. I am sure that for

---

[1] The relevant linguistic facts are as follows:

POIEIN. There is no doubt that this verb is used frequently in the LXX in a cult or sacrificial sense. Gore says there are from 60 to 80 instances. Here are some examples. Exod., xxix, 38ff: 'This is that which thou shalt "offer" (*poieseis*) upon the altar, two lambs. . . .' The word is repeated in the verses which follow. Again, I Kings, xi, 33, *epoiēsen tē Astartē*: in the A. V., 'they have worshipped Astoreth': but the LXX obviously means 'they sacrificed to Astarte'. It is also used of keeping the Passover: e.g. Matthew, xxvi, 18, and Western Text of Acts, xviii, 21. And it is possible that Luke ii, 27 means 'to sacrifice according to the custom of the law for him'.

ANAMNESIS. This is not the common word in LXX for a memorial before God in the sacrificial sense. The common word is *mnemosunon*, which we find in Mark xiv. 9, and Acts x., 4. But *anamnēsis* is sometimes found: Lev. xxiv, 7, 'frankincense . . . that it may be on the bread for a memorial' runs in the LXX 'and they shall be for loaves for a memorial (*eis anamnēsin*) lying before the Lord'. And Numb., x. 10: Your burnt offerings . . . and the sacrifices of your peace-offerings, that they may be to you for a memorial (*anamnēsis*) in the presence of your God'. Apart from the words of institution the only occurrence of *anamnēsis* in N.T. is Heb., x. 3, 'In these sacrifices there is every year a *remembrance* of sins'. This is ambiguous. See the passages collected with comments in Gore, *Body of Christ*, pp. 312ff, and Wotherspoon, *Religious Values in the Sacraments*, pp. 269ff.

St. Paul, who reports these words, the sacrament was much more than a festival of remembrance. And I do not think all the discussion of these words in recent times has gone for nothing or taught us nothing. I believe that, as we shall see before I have finished this lecture, the sacrament ought to contain for us something of this sense of a memorial before God of the sacrifice of Christ. But I do not think we can safely build upon a *sacrificial* interpretation of the words 'Do this for my *anamnēsis*.'

Nor do I think it is possible to find either in any New Testament passages or in the literature of our Reformed tradition, an actual interpretation of the sacrament as a sacrifice in anything like the sense which that holds in the Roman doctrine of the mass.

But yet I have entitled this lecture 'The Eucharistic Offering'; and I believe that phrase contains a profound and vital truth about the sacrament, a truth which we must rediscover, both for the enrichment of our own Christianity and for the sake of a deeper understanding with our sister churches in the ecumenical movement. And I believe that it is a truth which is very close to the New Testament understanding of Christianity and to the best and most Christian traditions of the Reformed Churches.

What, then, is the true and Christian idea of the eucharistic offering? I must lead you on by successive stages towards an answer.

I

In the first place, let us remember that all our worship may be regarded as an *offering* to God. And in this there is nothing in any way inconsistent with our Reformed tradition. Of course the strong reaction against Roman Catholic abuses of the idea of sacrifice, in the doctrine of the priest offering the body and blood of Christ as a sacrifice on the altar, has in some Protestant circles prejudiced every use of such words as 'priest', 'offering', 'oblation', 'sacrifice'; as if the very idea of our making an offering to God were uncongenial to true Christianity. Pagans make their offerings to God vainly imagining that such things can win His favour. The ancient Hebrews made their offerings to God, but these in themselves had no value: they simply pointed forward to Christ, and once He had come and made the once-for-all offering of Himself, sacrifices had no more place. There is nothing that we can offer: we can only receive what God offers us in Christ for our salvation. That sounds like good evangelical doctrine.

Yes: but alongside that let me place what the Westminster Shorter Catechism says in answer to the question, What is prayer? (and it is an answer which many a boy and girl in Scotland, and doubtless also in America, knew by heart in the days of our grandfathers): 'Prayer is an offering up of our desires unto God, for things agreeable to His will, in the name of Christ, with confession of our sins, and thankful acknowledgement of His mercies.'[1] Surely that is a very significant definition, and the more so, as it is found in so Reformed and Protestant a document as the Shorter Catechism. Prayer is not defined as *asking* for what we desire in order that we may receive it. It is the *offering-up* of our desires unto God. That is *sacrificial* language. And as in the ancient Hebrew ritual it is implied that it must be an *unblemished* sacrifice. It is not the mere uttering of any wishes we may have, but an offering up of our desires for things agreeable to God's will; and even then, because our desires are never all that they ought to be and are not worthy in themselves to be presented to God, they must be offered (the Catechism goes on to say) 'in the name of Christ', whose one eternal sacrifice, in which He is both priest and victim, is the basis of all Christian prayer.

II

In the next place let us note the use which the Westminster Confession makes of the word 'oblation' in treating of the sacrament of the Lord's supper. It is all the more significant

[1] Answer to Q. 98.

because it comes in the same breath as the violent condemnation of the 'Popish sacrifice of the mass'. 'In this sacrament Christ is not offered up to His Father, nor any real sacrifice made at all for remission of sins of the quick or dead; but only a commemoration of that one offering up of Himself, upon the cross, once for all, *and a spiritual oblation of all possible praise unto God for the same.*'[1] 'Oblation' means offering or sacrifice, and here we have the recognition of an oblation to God in the sacrament. It is an oblation of praise, of thanksgiving, which is the very meaning of the word 'eucharist' (*eucharistia*). It is the Christian counterpart of what in the Old Testament is repeatedly called 'the sacrifice of thanksgiving'.[2]

It is perhaps surprising that the Westminster divines did not here include in their footnotes a scripture reference to a New Testament passage which surely no reader in the first century could read without thinking of the eucharistic sacrifice. It is in the thirteenth chapter of the Epistle to the Hebrews. 'We have an altar from which those who serve the tabernacle have no right to eat. For the bodies of those animals whose blood is brought into the sanctuary by the high priest as a sacrifice for sin are burned outside the camp. So Jesus also suffered outside the gate in order to consecrate the people through his own blood. Therefore let us go forth to him outside the camp, bearing his reproach. For here we have no lasting city, but we seek the city which is to come. Through him then let us continually offer up to God a sacrifice of praise, that is, the fruit of lips that acknowledge his name. And do not forget beneficence and sharing, for with such sacrifices God is well pleased.'[3] It is not that last note that I want to dwell on now (as I shall return to it) but the one just before— *the sacrifice of praise*. All this is written, as you see, in the context of altar and priest and sacrifice, and the blood of the victim and the blood of Christ and our profession of His service, with its reproach, and our confession of His name in worship. And at the very heart and

[1] Chapter XXIX, 2.
[2] Cf. Lev. vii, 12ff; xxii, 29; Psalm cvii, 22; cxvi, 17; Amos iv, 5.
[3] Verses 10–15.

climax of it comes the idea of a 'eucharistic sacrifice' in the sense of an offering or oblation of praise to God through Christ.

III

In the third place, we shall all agree that in the sacrament we offer *ourselves* to God. That is part of the meaning of the eucharistic offering. And it means bringing the whole of our life and offering it to God: all that we are, all that we do, all that we possess. So it includes all our giving. Let us now recall the last sentence in that passage in the Epistle to the Hebrews: about doing good and sharing with others, because God is well pleased with such sacrifices. And let us recall the original meaning of the word 'offertory'. In the early centuries of the Christian Church, when the faithful came to the eucharist, they actually brought with them their offerings of bread and wine to be laid on the altar and then used as the elements in the sacrament: and that was the offertory. It is still done as regards the bread in the Eastern Church, and I have seen it at a celebration in a Russian Orthodox Church in Paris. That practice must have helped the faithful to feel that they were bringing the *common life* into God's presence, with its common tasks of ploughing and sowing and reaping and threshing and baking and all the other work that went to the making of bread.

We live in a much more complicated world, but we also, when we come to Communion, bring the offering of ourselves, our work, our play, our gifts, our powers, our possessions, our lives, that we may reconsecrate all to God. Ultimately that is the only offering which we can ever make—*the offering of ourselves*. And while in the sacrament it is profoundly true that God is the giver and we are the receivers, it is also true that receiving God means giving ourselves to Him; and indeed as we shall presently see, God's giving of Himself to us and our giving of ourselves to Him are but two ways of describing the same thing.

And so in our Church of Scotland Book of Common Order (as in the Book of Common Prayer of the Church of England) in the Prayer of Consecration, after we have asked God to sanctify the bread and wine to be the communion of the body and blood of Christ, and have offered to God our sacrifice of thanksgiving, we go on to *offer ourselves*: 'And here we offer and present to Thee ourselves, our souls and bodies, to be a reasonable, holy, and living sacrifice.'

IV

In the fourth place let us remember that we could not do this at all but for Christ; that we can only make an offering in union with Christ's eternal sacrifice. Our prayers are unworthy, *we* are unworthy, our praises are unworthy. How then can we offer ourselves, our prayers and praises to God? We can do it only through Christ. And whenever we make to God our offering of prayer, of praise, of self, we remind ourselves of that offering that Christ made of Himself, without which we could not come at all; that sacrifice which has opened up for us a new and living way into the Holy Place.

Perhaps we Protestants need especially to learn that lesson in the matter of our intercessions. How can we make intercession to God at all for other people and for good causes and for enterprises in the world? We know so little, we care so little, our prayers are so feeble, so isolated. What difference can they make in this great world? But what if we bring them to God in the name of Christ, remembering His great sacrifice for the salvation of the whole world, remembering also that 'He ever liveth to make intercession for us'; and thus pleading His eternal sacrifice, and uniting our intercessions with His?

What then is our relation to that sacrifice of Christ's when we are at the Lord's table? Is it simply a looking back, a memory?

It is indeed a looking back, a memory, and as we have already seen, that is very close to the heart of Christianity as a historical religion. *But is there not a profound sense in which the sacrifice of Christ, made once on Calvary, is an eternal sacrifice?* Here we touch the mystery of time and eternity, a mystery which enters into almost every theological problem. The very essence of incarnation, and indeed of all revelation, is the coming of eternity into the midst of time. God inhabits eternity, He cannot be limited by time. His existence transcends the distinction between past, present and future in an eternal present. God bore our sins incarnate in the passion and cross of Christ in one moment of history. But we cannot say that God's bearing of sin was confined to that moment. In some sense it is an eternal activity or passion of God's, and it has its direct 'vertical' relation to every moment of our sinful human history; so that the sins which we commit this very day are being borne and expiated by the eternal love of God.

One way of expressing this is by saying that the reconciling work of our great High Priest, who offered Himself on Calvary, goes on for ever at the heavenly altar in the Holy Place beyond the veil. This is the aspect which appears very prominently in the Epistle to the Hebrews. According to that Epistle the high-priestly work of Christ did not end with His death on the cross, but rather *began* with His death. His life on earth was a preparation, and then in His death on the cross He entered as our High Priest into the heavenly Holy Place, beyond the veil, where His priestly work goes on for ever; a continual offering of Himself to God on behalf of men. (And surely we must make a connection between that eternal self-offering of Christ in heaven and what we do in the sacrament of holy communion).

This line of thought has been pursued by theologians of many traditions in the modern world as a kind of rediscovery, and it was very notably developed sixty years ago by the Scottish Presbyterian divine Dr. William Milligan. After showing that the true conception of sacrifice is not so much the offering of death as the offering of life, he goes on to speak as follows of Christ's sacrifice: 'As an offering of life, it possesses the power of a present offering, not merely of an offering made and presented for us nineteen centuries ago, but of one which ascends even now for us before God, as much an offering as ever it was.' 'One of the greatest elements of Christ's sacrifice is, that it was not only made at a special moment of the past, a sacrifice to be ever afterwards remembered and pleaded; but that as an offering continually presented to the Father, it has a present sacrificial efficacy as powerful always as it was at the very first.'[1]

There is deep truth in these words; and surely we shall agree that only in union with that eternal sacrifice can we bring to God the offering of our unworthy prayers, our unworthy praises, our unworthy selves.

Now if we gather together all that we have been thinking about the Real Presence of Christ in the sacrament, about the offering that we make to God in the sacrament, and about the eternal sacrifice of Christ whose high-priestly work continues for ever at the heavenly altar, may we not say something like this: that in the sacrament, Christ Himself being truly present, He unites us by faith with His eternal sacrifice, that we may plead and receive its benefits and offer ourselves in prayer and praise to God? If we can say this, then surely we Protestants, we Presbyterians, have our doctrine of eucharistic sacrifice.

We need not be at all surprised that our Reforming fore-fathers reacted strongly against the medieval doctrine and practice of the sacrifice of the mass, and condemned it as 'injurious to Christ's one and only sacrifice on Calvary'. But it may be that the violence of that reaction has in the past blinded many of us to certain precious truths which ought never to have been lost. And there is no doubt that the best Roman Catholic divines of our own time, while of course teaching many things about the sacrament which we must still repudiate, cannot be accused of minimizing the one sacrifice of Christ on Calvary, but rather build everything upon it. An outstanding example is Eugene Masure's *The Christian Sacrifice*, from which I have already quoted. It contains many things that would be most uncongenial to us, but over and over again it lays the greatest stress on the sacrifice of Christ on Calvary as a once-for-all offering which cannot and need not be repeated and on which the efficacy of every eucharist is based. 'The mass does not repeat the redemption which was once for all perfectly

[1] *The Ascension and Heavenly Priesthood of our Lord* (1891), pp. 142ff.

accomplished. But it allows us to enter into this great work of our salvation and to obtain its benefits.'[1] Or take this great imaginative passage: 'The historic cross was long ago removed from Golgotha, the executioners are dead, Annas, Caiaphas and Pilate are no longer there, and the body and blood of the Saviour, reunited to His soul, have been lifted up. But the victim remains eternally, in all the great reality of incarnate grief and religious love, keeping still in being the drama which governs and explains the whole world's history.'[2]

The Roman Church is so remote from us on many points of doctrine, and even so much outside the modern ecumenical movement, that our relationship with it does not directly concern us. But the Anglo-Catholics, and many of the Eastern Orthodox, are deeply involved with ourselves in the ecumenical movement and I am greatly concerned to show that on this matter of the eucharistic sacrifice they are not as far from us as they and we have sometimes supposed. Take this from the Anglican Canon Quick: 'The Eucharist . . . is the perpetual externalization in human ritual of the self-offering of Christ, which was once for all in fact externalized on Calvary, but is ever real in the inward and heavenly sphere.'[3] Again: 'In the Eucharist . . . we make before God an offering . . . which is one with Christ's present and eternal offering of Himself.'[4] Or take this from the Eastern Orthodox Nicolas Arseniev: In the eucharist, 'we are raised above our human, earthly plane to contemplate the perpetual self-offering of the Lamb of God before the face of the Father. He suffered once on earth and He offers continually His death to the Father on the heavenly altar. . . . Our eucharist is the true representation of His true and continuous sacrifice, once for all time offered on the earth—on Golgotha, and perpetually presented to the Father on our behalf in eternity'.[5]

[1] *The Christian Sacrifice*, English translation, p. 214. The French title is *Le Sacrifice du Chef*. Cf. also the same author's later work, *Le Sacrifice du Corps Mystique*.
[2] Ibid. p. 215.
[3] *The Christian Sacraments* (1927), p. 198.   [4] Ibid. p. 200.
[5] In *The Ministry and the Sacraments*, ed. Dunkerley (1937), p. 86.

Is there a great gulf between that and what we Presbyterians can say when we speak of making our oblations of worship to God and offering ourselves to Him in the sacrament, showing forth Christ's eternal sacrifice and pleading its benefits? Listen to these words written by John Calvin. After repudiating the Roman doctrine of the sacrifice of the mass, he goes on: 'Under the other kind of sacrifice, which we have called *eucharisticon*, are included all the offices of charity by which, when we embrace our brethren, we honour the Lord Himself in His members: and likewise all our prayers, praises, thanksgiving and everything we do in the service of God: all of which are dependent on the greater sacrifice by which we are consecrated in soul and body as holy temples to the Lord.'[1] Again: 'This kind of sacrifice is indispensable in the supper of the Lord, in which, while we commemorate and declare His death, and give thanks, we do no other than offer the sacrifice of praise. . . . For we do not appear in the presence of God with our oblations without an intercessor. Christ is our Mediator through whom we offer ourselves and all that we have to the Father. He is our High Priest, who, having entered into the celestial sanctuary, opens the way of access for us. He is our altar, upon which we place our oblations, that whatever we venture we may venture in Him. In a word, it is He that "hath made us kings and priests unto God".'[2]

There is no doubt that words like 'sacrifice' and 'priest' and 'altar' have been very decisive words in the controversies between different churches; but I sometimes think that we should find our differences becoming smaller if we could only penetrate beneath *words* to real things. Is it not well to remind ourselves that whenever we use these words in speaking of Calvary or of the heavenly altar, we are using them not in a quite literal but in a figurative sense? And that is true even though we believe that Christ is the reality of which all the Old Testament priesthoods and altars and sacrifices were but shadows.

[1] *Institutes*, Book IV, Chapter xviii, 16.
[2] Ibid. Book IV, Chapter xviii, 17.

Christ was not in the literal sense a priest, but a layman. His sacrifice was not in the literal sense a sacrifice, and the cross was not in the literal sense an altar. Nor is the Holy Place within the veil literally a shrine, nor is the heavenly altar literally an altar in a temple, for there is no temple in the Holy City whose temple is God Himself.

But all these expressions have a profound meaning which makes them indispensable; and when we penetrate to the real meaning, we come nearer to each other too in our sacramental theology. And perhaps it does not greatly matter that some of us, when we think of the holy communion, speak of the altar, and others speak of the holy table, while the Anglican Prayer Book uses both terms. It is not an altar in the old sense, nor is it a table for ordinary use. But it has a meaning which makes it a sign of the sacrifice of Christ and of the offering that we make to God (altar); and it also has a meaning which makes it a sign of the heavenly food with which Christ feeds us, when on earth we anticipate 'the marriage supper of the Lamb' (table). And these meanings are not really two but one.

The Catholic tradition has sometimes made a great deal of the two-way movement in the eucharist, the Godward and the manward movement, and it has sometimes built upon the shape of the liturgy in the ancient sacrificial system.

First there was the offering of the victim to God in sacrifice, and then there was the return movement, the giving up of portions of the burnt-offerings to the people in a sacrificial feast. So in the medieval Catholic tradition there were the two successive stages of the eucharist: first the sacrifice of the mass, an offering by man to God, and then the gift of the heavenly food, Christ giving His body and blood to the communicants. These two parts could even be separated entirely in time from each other.

Perhaps the deepest reason why we refuse to make that separation is because the two movements, properly understood, are not really two, but one. They are not merely inseparable, but indistinguishable; they are two sides of one spiritual process. All that becomes plain when we penetrate beneath words to things, and remind ourselves, as we have had to do more than once in the course of these lectures, that here we are moving entirely in the realm of spiritual and personal relationships.

When in the sacrament we plead the sacrifice of Christ and in union with Him offer ourselves to God, the whole of that process is a giving and receiving in one. It might indeed be urged that the receiving is *prior* to the giving, because the initiative is always with God and the response is ours. Yet it can hardly be said that there is a *temporal* sequence. The very giving of ourselves to God is a receiving of Him, and the very receiving of Him is already a giving of ourselves. There is no other way of receiving Him except by giving ourselves to Him: and there is no way of giving ourselves to Him except by receiving Him. Both of these are happening in every single process, in every moment when we are worshipping God; and the supreme instrument and medium of that double movement, all in one, is the sacrament which we call the eucharist, or the holy communion, or the Lord's supper. This is what our Reformed Theology has always meant when it taught that it is through faith that Christ is given to us in the sacrament, and that this faith is itself the gift of God. So when we approach God's holy altar with our offerings of faith and worship, it becomes also the Lord's table, where we receive the heavenly food of His grace, mercy and peace.

There is one other element of this sacrament that I must dwell on for a moment as I come to the end of my task. Let us ever remember that the sacrament of holy communion is not an individual but a corporate act. That is of central importance whether we think of it in its aspect of the eucharist sacrifice or in its aspect as the Lord's supper.

On the one hand, when we think of the eucharistic sacrifice, we must keep firm hold of the conception of the priestly office of the whole Church. Even if the word 'priest' became suspect in the Reformed tradition, on the ground that there is no altar and no sacrifice and therefore no priest, that does not exhaust what the Reformed tradition has to say about priesthood. It has always believed not only in the high priesthood of Christ but also in the priesthood of all believers. But the priesthood of all believers is not merely an individual thing—it is bound up with the corporate priestly office of the Church, as a royal priesthood, a kingdom of priests exercising priestly functions in the name of the Great High Priest. That priestly office may for certain functions of word and sacrament be concentrated in individuals who are set apart and ordained to the ministry. But it is not really individual ministers who celebrate sacraments; it is the whole Church in its corporate capacity as a royal priesthood bringing its offering through Christ to God.

And, on the other hand, when we think of this sacrament as the Lord's supper, that corporate aspect becomes even plainer still. It is very often said that one of the defects of Calvinist theology is that it gives a too individualistic conception of Christianity. I sometimes wonder where those who make this criticism get their evidence, or whether they have ever read Calvin's *Institutes* for themselves. We may also wonder, perhaps, whether they have been present at a Presbyterian celebration of the sacrament, and compared it with their own celebrations, in which, it may be, the individual communicant goes up to the altar-rail and receives the elements from the hands of an individual priest. We must admit that a false individualism in religion is a disease which in the nineteenth century affected all religious traditions, our own included. But Archbishop Brilioth who made a very learned and penetrating study of all the diverse doctrines and practices of the eucharist, and who is himself a Lutheran, has maintained that the most distinctive contribution of the Reformed tradition in this matter is its expression of the corporate aspect, the note of fellowship in the celebration of the sacrament.

When we Presbyterians celebrate communion we do not go up individually to the altar; we sit in our places together as at the Lord's table. We are gathered at the family board for a feast in fellowship, we pass the bread and the cup from hand to hand, receiving them from our neighbour and passing them on to our neighbour in the communion of the Lord's supper. What excuse then have we for forgetting that this is indeed a corporate act, a meal in sacred fellowship, an anticipation of 'the marriage supper of the Lamb'?

Unless our sacramental service maintains at its very heart that note of corporate worship, that note of Christian solidarity, of fellowship in the body of Christ, it will not be the holy communion at all. When St. Paul was writing to the Christians at Corinth about their abuses of this sacrament, he said very solemnly, 'He that eats and drinks, eats and drinks judgment to himself, if he discerns not the body'.[1] Many scholars have thought that what he means there by the body is not the flesh and blood of Christ, but the body of Christ in the sense of His Church. In the congregation at Corinth there were cliques and factions, individual self-assertion, lack of unity and fellowship in Christ, and their rivalries and jealousies sometimes appeared even in their Christian worship. How could such people worthily celebrate the Lord's supper? They were failing to discern the body, they had no due sense of the body to which they belonged, the one body of Christ. They were eating and drinking as selfish individuals, instead of offering to God as one body the sacrifice of thanksgiving or joining as one family in the corporate festival of the Lord's table.

But without that note of unity in Christ, fellowship with each other, in the corporate life of the one body, holy communion would not be holy communion at all, and the Church would not be the Church of Christ. May it not be that both the doctrine of the Real Presence and the doctrine of the eucharistic offering, begin to come right and to take their true shape when they are controlled by the idea of the sacrament as a corporate act of the one body of Christ?

[1] I Cor. xi, 29.

III

Philosophers and Theologians on the Freedom of the Will

Philosophers and Theologians on the Freedom of the Will[1]

I
t is a curious fact that while the problem of free will has been long and widely discussed by both philosophers and theologians in the modern world, it has been largely in two separate compartments, the one set seldom conferring with the other, or even overhearing what the other has to say. Sometimes they seem almost to be talking of two different things.

I

Among philosophers one may say that it has been 'orthodox' to assert and defend the freedom of the human will against those schools that would explain it away or show it to be impossible. On the whole, it has been the sceptical, materialistic or naturalistic philosophers that have denied the freedom of the will. If we take the three great ideas of God, Freedom and Immortality, we may say that it has usually been the philosophers who denied God and immortality that also denied freedom. And those who have defended freedom have usually done so in the interests of the higher life of man, because it seemed plain that if free will is an illusion, moral obligation is meaningless. The famous argument of Immanuel Kant was conceived

[1] Reprinted from the *Scottish Journal of Theology*, Vol. 4, No. 2, June 1951.

in that spirit. Starting with the consciousness of moral obligation as something which has immediate certainty, he proceeded to the conclusion that therefore there must be such a thing as freedom of the will by which a man *can* make the right choice. A man must be free to do what he *ought* to do; otherwise 'ought' becomes meaningless. This is the famous argument that 'ought' implies 'can'; moral obligation implies free will. It is in that spirit that philosophers have usually defended the freedom of the will, and those who have followed this line have done so with the air of being 'on the side of the angels'.

But when we turn from the philosophers to the theologians, especially those in the tradition of the Reformation, we find something surprisingly different. We find that the line of argument outlined above ('I ought, therefore I can') is very like what has been repudiated by theologians as the Pelagian heresy. The argument that 'I ought, therefore I can' is indeed precisely what Pelagius was teaching in opposition to St. Augustine. To St. Augustine the will of unregenerate man is so wholly enslaved by sin, that though he ought to obey God and keep His commandments, he is utterly unable to do so. The regenerate man is able to make the right choice, but it is entirely divine grace that enables him to do it, and this grace is omnipotent and irresistible. This may seem to leave no room at all for freedom. Yet St. Augustine does in fact defend free will against those who would deny it, because to him freedom of the will does not mean the *ability* to make the right choice. So man must be described as having free will, because whatever choice he makes, it is his own will that chooses, even if it is true that as unregenerate he *cannot* make the right choice. Thus, according to St. Augustine, man has free will in a sense, even when enslaved by sin.

But when we come to the Protestant Reformers, we find them actually denying free will to unregenerate man altogether, and claiming that they have St. Augustine with them. Martin Luther's famous work *De servo arbitrio*, written in refutation of the views of Erasmus, hotly and uncompromisingly denied the *liberum arbitrium* of which the Scholastics had spoken. Calvin, while allowing that a man acts voluntarily and not by compulsion, maintains that if that is all that can be said, it is not worthy of the name of free will, and he regards the use of the phrase as misleading and dangerous. Unregenerate man does not possess free will. His will is enslaved by sin, and he is unable to will what is good. It is this *inability* that he is chiefly concerned to emphasize, and here he can fairly claim that he has St. Augustine with him.

Now this is obviously the very opposite of what Kant was concerned to establish. It is a flat denial of the principle that 'ought implies can'. In many ears it sounds like a very perverse denial. But Professor Emil Brunner in our own time has gone even further, and maintained that 'ought' implies 'cannot'! 'If I feel I *ought* to do right, it is a sign that I cannot do it. If I could do it, there would be no question of "ought" about it at all. The sense of "ought" shows me the Good at an infinite impassable distance from my will.'[1] This brings to a sharp point the contention which has run through so much of the Protestant theological tradition, denying the very principle of Kant's argument for the freedom of the will.

I have heard it suggested that the truth of Kant's argument becomes clearer if we add a few words to it and say: 'I ought, therefore I can *if I choose*.' If that is what Kant meant, then everybody would agree with him. Then his dictum would mean merely that there cannot be a moral obligation to perform an act which is physically impossible, such as rescuing a drowning man when one cannot swim oneself, or escaping from a prison camp when one is bound with chains. In that sense all would agree that there is no 'ought' except in cases where I *could* do the thing *if I chose*. But it is impossible to reconcile the parties in that way, because that is not what Kant meant. He meant: I ought *to choose* this, therefore I *can choose it*. To him the good will was what mattered. The moral act was the act of *choice*. And what he meant by the assertion of freedom was that

---

[1] Emil Brunner, *The Divine Imperative* (Engl. tr.), p. 74. It is only fair to add that Brunner distinguishes between *formal* freedom, which every man possesses, and *material* freedom, which the enslaved will does not possess.

man is always free to make his choice between the good and the evil. Every man has at every moment the power to make the right choice. And that is precisely what the tradition of Protestant theology has condemned as the Pelagian heresy, maintaining that man is not free or able of himself to do what he ought to do.

It is easy to dismiss this paradoxical position as making nonsense of the moral life and of all moral responsibility. But it is not often noticed how the paradox appears to be borne out by the language that we normally and naturally use in describing certain moral situations. Let us imagine the case of a man who in a 'police state' is sent to prison for speaking out against injustice. That stops his activities for the time being, and so long as he is in prison he does not tell himself that he *ought* at once to return to the charge, for he *cannot* do that, as he is a prisoner. But then he is released from prison, and he knows he ought to take up the struggle again and speak out. Let us suppose, further, that he finds he has not the courage to do it. He *ought* but he *cannot* bring himself to do it, though he is physically free. And looking back afterwards, he says: 'I know I ought to have done it, but I simply couldn't.' Any one of us might quite naturally use similar language any day about some lapse of courage in some difficult situation yesterday. 'I *ought* to have acted, but when the moment came, I hadn't the courage, I couldn't do it.' Do we mean that kind of language seriously? If not, why do we so naturally use it? But if we do mean it, we are acknowledging situations in which 'ought' does not imply 'can', in which in some sense we are not free to make the right choice.

Moreover, there are other situations in which we say that a man is not free to make the wrong choice. If a good man whom we know well is accused of a very mean and dishonourable action, we say: 'I do not believe he did it: he *could not* do such a thing, he is quite *incapable* of such a base action.' If we mean that seriously, as I believe in some sense we do, we imply that a man, in so far as he is a good man (and of course it is a matter of degree) is incapable of doing evil. He lacks the freedom to make the wrong choice.

If these things are true, we are left with the question: where does freedom come in? What area of life remains for the operation of what philosophers and theologians have called free will? And what *is* freedom of the will?

II

All this suggests that there must be different senses of 'free will', or perhaps we should say different kinds or degrees of freedom. And of course we are not the first to make that discovery. Let us look at some of the ways in which a distinction has been drawn between different sorts or grades of freedom.

(*a*) The most famous distinction of all is that which goes back to St. Augustine, between the lesser freedom of *posse non peccare* and the greater freedom of *non posse peccare*. The lesser freedom, by which a man is able to avoid sinning, though he is also able to sin, Augustine ascribed to man before the Fall. The greater freedom of being unable to sin at all he ascribed to redeemed man in heaven, and primarily of course to God, who can only act according to His nature, which is wholly good, and who therefore cannot sin. Whatever freedom may be possessed by unregenerate fallen man on earth, in St. Augustine's view, it is not either of these kinds.

(*b*) There is a certain similarity between this distinction and the well-known distinction made by the Cambridge philosopher Henry Sidgwick in 1888 between 'Good' or 'Rational Freedom' and 'Neutral' or 'Moral Freedom'.[1] Sidgwick pointed out that in Kant's treatment of the subject the word 'freedom' is used in two distinct senses, both of which are quite legitimate, though Kant shows no consciousness of the difference between them. *Neutral* freedom is the freedom which all men equally possess (as implied in the moral imperative), and which is shown in bad actions just as much as in good actions: it is simply the capacity to choose between different courses of action, a capacity without which, we may say, a will would not be a will at

[1] In an article in *Mind*, reprinted as an Appendix to the 6th edition of Sidgwick's *The Methods of Ethics*.

all, and a man would not be a man. But when Kant proceeds to analyse freedom and to show how it is possible, he betrays that now he is using the word in a different sense and thinking of a different freedom—the freedom of rationality, exhibited only in good volitions, in which the will is moved by reason, free from the domination of passions and inclinations. This is *good* or *rational* freedom. Sidgwick points out incidentally that there is a third sense which is sometimes given to freedom of the will—that which he indicates by the term 'Capricious Freedom'. He is thinking of those 'Libertarian' philosophers (including the Scottish Thomas Reid) who conceived of freedom as 'the power of acting without a motive', and who tried to maintain its reality in that sense.

(c) A still more elaborate and comprehensive analysis, which in a manner covers these two distinctions and more, is made from a theological point of view in the ninth chapter of the *Westminster Confession of Faith* (1647). It begins by giving, as a general background, a statement of the freedom which man always possesses as man, and which continues through all his changing states—the state of innocence, the state of sin, the state of grace, and the state of glory. 'God hath endued the will of man with that natural liberty, that it is neither forced, nor by any absolute necessity of nature determined, to good or evil.' That is the minimal kind of freedom which Luther and Calvin did not consider worthy of the name at all. To say that the will has this freedom is no more than saying that it is a will, and without it a man would not be a man.

Against that general background there are four stages. In the first, 'the state of innocency' (sometimes called 'original righteousness'), man 'had freedom and power to will and to do that which is good and well pleasing to God; but yet mutably, so that he might fall from it'. This is the freedom of *posse non peccare*, the initial stage (whether we conceive it in a historico-temporal or in a mythical and ideal way) in which man could choose either good or evil, and from which, though he actually fell, he *might not* have fallen.

The second stage gives us 'the state of sin' (sometimes called 'the state of nature'), in which man, now a fallen creature, is utterly unable to will what is good or to convert himself from evil. He is free only in the minimal sense of having a will. His will is not free in any substantial sense, but enslaved. That is the *servum arbitrium.*

The third stage is the state of grace. A man is now freed from his bondage, and can freely choose and will what is good, though he does not always do it, because there is still evil in him which can lead him astray. And in so far as he does over-come evil and choose good, it is not his own resources that enable him. It is the grace of God that enables him; not by compelling him, but by making him willing, so that he freely wills what is good. This is the highest freedom open to man on earth; and it is not the freedom of independence.

The fourth stage described in the chapter is the state of glory. 'The will of man is made perfectly and immutably free to do good alone in the state of glory only.' This is plainly identical with the *maxima libertas* of the *non posse peccare*, the inability to sin described by St. Augustine; and as here ascribed to re-deemed man in the final beatitude of heaven, it is of course not regarded as man's achievement, but as something wrought in him by God.

III

I have indicated some of the well-known attempts that have been made to distinguish different senses or kinds or degrees of freedom of the will, and it is difficult to relate them to each other; so that the total effect is perhaps one of extreme con-fusion. I am not able entirely to clear up the confusion of this endlessly difficult subject, but I wish now to suggest some simple truths which seem to emerge.

(1) The freedom of the human will does not mean sheer indetermination. In its minimal sense it means that man in his behaviour functions differently from lower organisms in that he functions by choosing, he acts by choice. Whether a man is good or bad, whether he does right or wrong, there is a sense

in which he does it freely, at least in the case of a great many of his actions, all those which from the moral point of view can be regarded as the man's 'acts'. He acts freely in the sense that he does what he chooses to do. Someone will argue that the man chooses according to his nature, his character; and that, being such as he is, he could not choose differently. But if that is true, it does not make the man's action any less his own, or make him less responsible for it. For his nature, his character, is not something other than himself, compelling him from outside. His character is himself. That is what he is. So it is *he* that determines his actions.

It is quite misleading to speak of this position as 'determinism', and the use of that word is a frequent source of confusion. The word is often used in such a way as to suggest that the determinist is perversely or sorrowfully denying something which would make life more significant if it could be affirmed, and that he is reducing the human will to a mechanical level, to the disadvantage of moral responsibility. Such determinism is absurd. But on the other hand we do not help matters by introducing the 'capricious freedom', as Sidgwick called it, of 'action without a motive'. That is what would really be mechanical, for the action of a machine is indeed action without a 'motive'. And in the realm of will such 'libertarianism' or 'indeterminism' would seem to make human actions, from the moral point of view, purely contingent, fortuitous, unconnected with the character of the agent, because unmotivated. That would be the very acme of irresponsibility. Surely we are responsible for our actions precisely because they do not spring 'out of the blue', utterly undetermined and accidental, but spring from what we are, by a kind of determination quite different from the chains of mechanical causation which determine the behaviour of material things; it is the determination of personal choice.

(2) It seems plain, though it sounds paradoxical, that this freedom of the will which we all possess does not necessarily carry with it the *ability* to do or be what we ought to do or be. There is a sense in which a man may be unable to will what he

ought to will. It is difficult to get this point clear, and at first it seems contrary to common sense. Indeed a moralist may very well argue that if a man's will is bent in a wrong direction, only the man himself, by his own will, can put it right. Yet the situation is not so simple. How can the will put the will right? How could it put anything right unless it were already right itself? When the will is wrong, it does not *wish* to put itself right: that is what is wrong with it, since it is a will.

This becomes particularly plain when we remember the obvious principle that what matters morally is not simply the action or even the intention, but the motive and therefore the whole bent of the character. The divine imperative says to me: Thou shalt love thy neighbour as thyself. And yet I cannot *make* myself love my neighbour. It is impossible to evade this difficulty by saying with Kant that what is commanded is merely 'practical love' in the sense of 'beneficence for duty's sake'. I ought, surely, not only to deal justly and kindly with my neighbour, but to *love* my neighbour; and if I do not, that is something of which I ought to be ashamed. And yet I cannot put it right by an act of will. If I am a selfish, loveless man, if I am self-centred (which is the root of all evil), how could I possibly draw myself out of my self-centredness and make myself love other people? The more I try to improve my character, the more am I concentrating on myself, and that is not a cure for self-centredness. Apparently I cannot cure it. And yet I know that is blameworthy. I know that I am responsible for it, and that I ought to love my fellows though I cannot. Thus, though as a human being I have the minimal kind of freedom described above, there is a sense in which I am not free to do what I ought to do. There is moral obligation without 'ability' to choose the good. That is why the theologians used to speak so much not only of freedom but of 'ability' and 'inability', and that is why they spoke of the *servum arbitrium*.

(3) Is it then true that in order to reach the genuine freedom we have to pass beyond morality? Is it possible that we cannot unravel this tangle of the problem of free will until we introduce the factor which theologians have intended when they have

spoken of divine grace? 'Thou shalt love thy neighbour as thyself'—that sums up the Christian ethic. But the central tradition of Christian theology has always taught that it is not in human nature, as we know it on earth, to obey that commandment. We cannot even begin to do it by an exercise of our own wills. We can only do it when grace comes to our aid. Now what does that mean? Is it only a piece of theological jargon or mystification? Or is it a profound and vital truth?

Every student of philosophy is familiar with what is called 'the paradox of hedonism', the unquestionable fact that if one seeks pleasure as the *summum bonum*, one does not obtain it, that the quest of happiness defeats itself. But (as I have elsewhere pointed out) there is another paradox which is not so often noticed: what we may call 'the paradox of moralism', the fact that the quest of *goodness* defeats itself. It is not precisely by trying to make ourselves into good men that we become good men. It is not by careful cultivation of our characters in the light of an ideal that the finest character is actually formed. That purely moralistic method is apt to lead either to manifest failure or, if it seems to be succeeding, to a self-righteous pride, which is really the worst failure of all. It is 'Pharisaism'. That is how the quest of goodness defeats itself.

The true saints have followed a different way. Instead of concentrating on their own characters, they have been God-centred. They have been less conscious of themselves than of God, less conscious of an ethic or an ideal than of the will of God, the love of God, which called out the response of their faith and love. Thus they have slowly and gradually come to love their neighbours in God. And, looking back, they have regularly confessed that whatever good was in their lives was not their own achievement but was due to divine grace. Not that this involved any cramping of their own personality, or destruction of their own freedom. Rather they would confess that never were they so truly free as in those moments when they were most wholly dependent on the grace of God. It seems plain, then, that there is a quite luminous and practical truth underlying the mysterious statement that only by the aid of divine grace can a man be free to do and be what he ought to do and be. It means at least this, as a mere matter of psychological description: that the best kind of living, or the finest type of character, does not come through sheer volitional effort to realize an ideal, but in a more indirect way, as the fruit of a life of faith in God. And if the saints are right in their account of this, it means that we are not truly free except when we are depending on the grace of God.

These conceptions are indeed full of difficulties for the theologian as well as for the philosopher, and raise further questions which would lead us far beyond the scope of this article. I believe there is something fundamentally paradoxical about the mystery of the human will. But I think we have got so far as to be able to see through what is a common over-simplification of the whole matter. People often think of the moral life as if it were a case of man as a rational being, with a perfectly free will, confronted with moral choices from moment to moment, and always having the power to make the right choice, though he does not always do it. Thus they imagine that free will in itself is quite simple, and that contradictions arise only when we introduce the conception of the action of divine grace, which seems inconsistent with human freedom. But that is really a naïve and unrealistic falsification of the picture. Free will is not so simple. No doubt every will possesses 'neutral freedom' in a sense which amounts to no more than saying that it is a will, and there is no contradiction between this freedom and the conception of divine grace properly understood as 'a gracious personal relationship' (Oman). But there is a further freedom which, so far from being confused or contradicted by the conception of grace, cannot be explained without that conception. It appears to be true in a very plain and practical sense that a man is not really free to live as he ought to live until he passes beyond a self-contained morality into that relationship which the saints have described as dependence on the grace of God.

IV

The Preaching of the Christian Doctrine

AN ADDRESS TO MINISTERS

The Preaching of the Christian Doctrine

The only thing that could justify me in addressing you on this subject is the fact that you invited me to do so and that, being invited, I hardly had the right to refuse. As one of those set apart by the Church for the study and teaching of theology, I have a duty to the whole Church and could not well decline to speak to a body such as this on such a subject. I need hardly say that I do not come as one who knows more about it than you do: indeed, when it comes to the *preaching* of doctrine, I have no doubt that some of you know far more than I, and can put it into far better practice. And it is a somewhat invidious matter for one who, like myself, is no longer engaged in the regular weekly ministry of preaching to a congregation, to come from outside and address you, my brother ministers, on *any* aspect of preaching.

There is, however, one positive reason why I was glad when I was invited to tackle this problem. The reason is that I am convinced, and have long been convinced, that we ought to be preaching Christian doctrine much more than we are. I have sometimes said, during the last dozen years, that when I look back to the days of my regular pastoral ministry, one of the things I regret is that I did not more faithfully try to make my ministry a *teaching* ministry; and that if I had to begin again I would set myself to give more definite *teaching* from the pulpit.

Once when I said that in seminar to my students at St. Andrews one of them asked whether that wasn't merely because, now that I had grown accustomed as a professor to teaching theology, I was apt to see things from that point of view and to wish to play the professor even in the pulpit. That was perhaps a very penetrating question, but I do not think the answer is in the affirmative. There is more to it than that. I believe, indeed, that there is a great difference between what a professor of theology ought to be doing in his classes and what a preacher (perhaps that very same professor) ought to be doing in his pulpit; and it would be a dreadful mistake for the latter to adopt precisely the same method and technique as the former. That is perhaps why so many theological professors, who may once have been fairly good preachers, become very dull and heavy in the pulpit, a weariness to the flesh of the man in the pew! But that is a matter of method, and I am convinced that the preacher, while always remembering that he *is* a preacher to the great mixed body of the people, ought also to be a teacher; and still more he must remember that what he has to preach is not simply whatever fancies or even whatever great thoughts come into his head, but *the Christian message*—and that really means Christian doctrine.

Moreover, I think that lesson is specially needful for a Church like ours, a Presbyterian Church, in contrast to some others. What I mean is this. Some Churches, like the Church of England, are far more fully liturgical than ours, and also have a far fuller observance of the Christian year; and that in itself is a continual training in Christian belief. A devout Anglican knows his Prayer Book through and through: knows it probably much better than he knows his Bible, and much better than we know the Bible. And the Prayer Book is built, in its whole structure and all its details, on Christian doctrine. Moreover the devout Anglican, particularly if he be Anglo-Catholic, follows the stages of the Christian year as faithfully and as naturally as a farmer follows the seasons and months of the agricultural year, each with its particular tasks in the fields and the steading, and all in a definite order which is not subject to any major change. And thus as surely as the good farmer comes to know and understand the ways of nature until they have become part of the very habit of his mind, so the good Catholic comes to know something of the ways of super-nature, until they also are part of himself—and these are just what is summed up in Christian belief, Christian doctrine. The same thing is perhaps even more true of the Eastern Orthodox Church than of the Anglican. The Eastern Church has hardly any explicit teaching of the people, and it may therefore seem to be a very undoctrinal Church. But its divines tell us that for their Church the doctrine is enshrined in the liturgy and the ritual and that is how it gets into the hearts of the people. They even tell us that to them the word 'orthodox' does not mean 'right belief' so much as 'right worship'—*doxa*, not in the sense of *opinion* or *belief* but in the sense of *glory:* right glory or right worship. Thus they would claim that it is through the dramatic means of the liturgy and its ritual moving on through the sequence of the Christian year that the people come to know in their hearts and minds what Christianity is. *Lex orandi, lex credendi.*

Now a Church like the Church of Scotland has in the past been accustomed to provide for that need in a different way, a much more theological way—by definitely doctrinal, even theological, preaching; so that wherever one goes one finds that people speak with respect of Scottish Christianity as really having a theology, and taking theology very seriously, even in the ordinary life of the Church. One wonders sometimes whether Scotland is not now living upon its reputation in that respect. Do we not often get the impression that a great many people, not only outsiders but regular members and attenders of our Church in Scotland, are extraordinarily hazy as to what Christian teaching really is—as to what Christians believe or are expected to believe. It may seem indeed that Scotland has somewhat disastrously fallen between two stools. In the seventeenth century we largely gave up liturgical worship and the observance of the Christian year, and trusted instead to the strong meat of doctrinal preaching. But now the latter also has gone by the board, because all kinds of developments of thought in the modern world made it too difficult to sustain; so that the Christian people of Scotland, the Church folk of Scotland, are very hazy about, often very ignorant of, essential Christian belief.

But also I am inclined to think many of them are beginning to pine for more knowledge. I am sure that is true in the student world. In recent years I have seen more of students—of various faculties—than I have of any other class of people; and I have seen many signs of this. A great many students are feeling and saying: we don't really know what Christianity is, or what it teaches, but we very much want to know. In recent years students of all faculties have been talking of these things a great deal among themselves, sitting up in each others' rooms to all hours discussing matters of belief. And they are also willing, and sometimes even eager, to listen to addresses on such subjects. If the same is true of church-folk generally— of the people who attend our services—that gives us at the present time a very special opportunity and responsibility to preach Christian doctrine.

How, then, are we to set about it? I shall occupy the remainder of my time in giving a series of suggestions on that point.

(1) In the first place, we can preach doctrine *incidentally* all the time. I mean that apart from any special series, and whatever text we may have for our sermon, we can make sure that we are using it to declare the authentic Christian message, and that *implies* Christian doctrine. Perhaps that is the best way of all, though it is not enough in itself. Perhaps it is the best way of all, as a continuous basis for the rest, because, instead of extracting the doctrine and presenting it in *abstracts*, this method makes the doctrine to arise naturally out of some story or passage of Scripture. I think the great danger, when we set ourselves to the duty of preaching doctrine, is that we should become too theological, and use theological jargon, and merely bamboozle people by giving them some theological construction that doesn't seem to have much bearing on the lives they

have to live day by day. We *must* try to be concrete and even practical in our treatment. This is why I say that perhaps the incidental method is the best of all. But it is not enough by itself. It might be, if we were all at the same time first-class theologians and first-class preachers (such as, e.g., Reinhold Niebuhr); if we were all so richly endowed that we could continually clothe the skeleton of doctrine with the warm flesh and blood of living human experience, so that our hearers could, as it were, feel the bones of doctrine without seeing them as bare bones. Then the incidental way of preaching Christian doctrine would be enough. But very few of us are equal to that test. We cannot trust ourselves so far. We must have a more definite and systematic method, if we are to do justice to Christian doctrine.

(2) In the second place, then, a further step is to base our preaching on the observance of the Christian year. I pointed out a few minutes ago that the Churches that observe the Christian year more fully have an advantage over us in this matter. But there is no reason why we should allow them to have this advantage. And indeed we are beginning to catch up with them . The observance of the Christian year in our Churches has advanced very greatly since the days when my ministry began, and I believe we ought to advance it still further. There is a special advantage in basing our preaching of doctrine on the Christian year. It enables us to present the various doctrines as making up an organic whole instead of letting them stand apart. After all, the Christian message is more than an agglomeration of separate doctrines. It is more even than a *system* of doctrines. It is a *story* that has to be told and explained. When we observe the Christian year, from Advent through Christmas and Epiphany, Lent, Passiontide and Easter, Ascensiontide, Whitsuntide and Trinity, on to another Advent, we are in a sense living that story over again; this gives us the opportunity of explaining its elements (its doctrines) in a temporal sequence; which is their true sequence, because the Christian message is the Christian story. Thus it seems to me that every consideration both of sound theology

and of sound psychology points us to a fuller use of the Christian times and seasons in the preaching of doctrine.

Moreover, let me say in passing, I would include here not only the times and seasons of the Christian year, but other special times as well, in particular the sacramental seasons. I am convinced that the people of the Church need far more teaching than we have been accustomed to give them on the sacraments of baptism and the Lord's supper; and surely the time to give them that teaching is the time when these sacraments are actually being observed. As regards baptism I am sure you will agree with me that a great many of our faithful church-folk are in a state of complete fog about its meaning —which is a dreadful condition of affairs. It has always been my own practice to speak a few words about its meaning as part of the baptismal service every time I have baptized a child, whether in church or in a private house. And I believe it is only by that constant method of interpretation at the psychological moment that we can give our people a sound sense of what baptism means. And as regards the Lord's supper, I have long been of opinion that we ought at communion seasons to preach much more *directly* about the sacrament. At the preparatory service and at the actual communion service it has been a common thing to preach on any more or less central topic of the Christian Gospel. But why don't we more often preach directly on some aspect of the sacrament itself? Surely our people need it. Surely there is a widespread confusion and ignorance even within the Church about the meaning of the Lord's supper. Of course we give our young communicants careful teaching about it; but we cannot be so naïve as to imagine that that is more than a tiny beginning, on which they could not stand an examination a month later. The thing needs to be done over and over again with both repetition and variety, and surely it is best done at sacramental seasons—not in the form of a theological lecture, but with all the simplicity and vividness that we can command—if only we make sure that we are giving the truly Christian interpretation.

(3) But now I must go a step further. I have pointed out

two ways of preaching doctrine: the incidental way, and the way based on 'times and seasons'. But I believe there is room for a method which goes beyond both of these: I mean the more systematic method of giving definite *courses* of sermons on the great doctrines. There are a good many parts of Christian doctrine which are not naturally covered by the scheme of the Christian year—creation, providence, election, the Christian doctrines of man, sin, forgiveness, prayer, the Church; and even those which definitely come into the Christian year need to be sometimes more fully expounded. If generally we are observing the Christian year, perhaps the best time for such a course is in the longer sequence of Sundays after Trinity. But of course you know better than I do that such a course should not be made too long; and so it may be fitted into either morning or evening service at various times of year.

Now this is obviously where we touch the whole problem at its most difficult. This is where we are most in danger of doing this task but not doing it well. Perhaps a professional theologian like myself is more in danger of that than any of you, because I am more apt to see things from the point of view of the theological classroom than from that of the plain man in the pew who is not a theologian. Therefore, why should I be addressing you on the subject? But since I am, and since I have been expressing my conviction that the preaching of doctrine is much needed, it is my duty now to go on to make some suggestions as to how we can best aim at avoiding the mistakes and failures and showing ourselves to be sound workmen, rightly dividing the word of truth for the edification of the Church.

(a) In the first place I should like to suggest that our preaching of doctrine should be truly Biblical, not simply in the sense that we should be true to Bible teaching, but that as a matter of method in preaching we should let the doctrine spring out of the Bible. That has more than one advantage. It has of course the fundamental advantage of securing that the doctrine we preach shall be sound doctrine. For whatever be our theory of Scripture and our theological attitude to it—whether we are fundamentalists or liberals or Barthians or anything else—we shall all agree that the Bible interpreted in the light of Christ must be the touchstone of our doctrine. And we do need that touchstone in actual practice. For it is perfectly possible for a minister, even after all his theological training, to preach things which from the point of view of the Christian message are simply false doctrine, unsound and un-Christian teaching. It is quite possible to do that even when one has taken a text from the Bible and used it as the starting-point. When I say that our preaching of doctrine should be Biblical, I do not mean simply that the sermon should be hung upon a particular text, but that it should be based upon genuine Biblical study— the kind of Biblical study that ought to be going on all the time in the lives of us who are ministers of the Word, the kind of Biblical study which is a continual endeavour to understand the Christian message as expressed in its classical documents. That, I say, will keep our teaching sound.

But then that Biblical method of preaching has a second advantage. It will help the people to understand and use the Bible for themselves. It is only a fraction of what we say in any one sermon that even the keenest of our people can remember. But if we use the Bible aright in our preaching, so that light breaks out from it, some people at least will learn how to read the Bible, so that they can go on learning from the fountain-head for themselves.

I suppose that now I ought to give an example of how a sermon on doctrine may be made to spring out of Scripture. Let us imagine that we are writing a sermon for Trinity Sunday. It may well seem that this is the most difficult doctrine of all to preach from the pulpit; and it may occur to some of you to remind me that this can hardly be called a Biblical doctrine at all in its developed form, though the materials for it are in the Bible. Yet I believe this doctrine to be almost more than any other a doctrine that must, for pulpit purposes, be made to spring from Scripture.

I think it might be done like this. I would begin by pointing out the simple fact, so often forgotten in common religious speech, that the doctrine of the Trinity is not simply a doctrine of a divine Trio, but a doctrine of *one* in three, of three Persons, Father, Son and Holy Spirit, in One God. *One God:* that is the starting-point, the background. And so you may begin your sermon by showing in a few sentences how the whole of the Old Testament may be regarded as an epitome of how Israel slowly learnt her lesson that God is One. 'Look unto me and be ye saved, all ye ends of the earth, for I am God, and there is none else.' That was a great revelation, something gained that must never again be lost. The splendid redemptive news of the One God who rules the whole world in righteousness and mercy—that was something that the New Testament inherited from the Old, and it could never go back on that.

But why couldn't Christianity be content with that? Why did it have to go on to something more mysterious, to something which may even seem to give up all that was gained as regards the unity of God, or which at least seems to add mystification to our whole belief in God? Why did it become necessary to go on to the doctrine that God is three in one, and one in three?

It was because something happened; and then something else happened. It was because of two tremendous new facts of history and experience, which compelled people to restate and enrich their doctrine of God.

First the fact of Jesus Christ. About nineteen centuries ago there appeared among the Jews in Palestine a working man called Jesus, who became a religious leader but soon got into trouble with the authorities and was condemned to death and crucified. But His followers were quite sure that God had raised Him from the dead and that He was alive. Nay, they were quite sure of something even more wonderful: that God Himself was *in* this Jesus, even when He died on the Cross. But how could that be? They could not simply *identify* this Jesus with God the Father Almighty, for Jesus spoke *about* God, and prayed to God; and Jesus was tempted, and then He died on the Cross, whereas God cannot be tempted, and God cannot die. What then were they to say about Jesus? Was He a second god, a lesser god, or a demigod, an intermediate being between God and man? No, certainly not. For there is only one God, and there are no demigods such as pagans believe in. Jesus was a real man. And yet they were sure it was God who had come to them in Jesus. What then were they to say about it? This is what they said: that this was the Word of God, or the Divine Logos, *incarnate* in human life. Or better still, because nothing was more characteristic of Jesus than His deep filial consciousness of God as Father, they said in explanation of Him that He was the Son of God, appearing in human life. Not that there were two gods, separate individuals, like a human father and son. And yet they had to speak of God the Father and God the Son. They meant something which they could not adequately express in words at all. For something so tremendous had come into their lives that it stretched all their language to breaking point. So they said new things about God: they spoke of the Father and the Son. They had to do it, because of this great new fact of history and experience: the fact of Jesus Christ.

But then something else happened. We may indicate it by the one word Pentecost. It was like this. The men who had known Jesus in the flesh, who had been His disciples, who had found God in Him, and who were always appalled and incredulous when He told them He was going to be taken away from them by a violent death, would have told you a few weeks afterwards that they had not lost their Master at all; that He had come back to them in a new and more wonderful and more spiritual way, to remain with them forever, a divine Presence in their midst and in their hearts. There was one great day in particular when this came home to them in an overpowering manner, on the date of the Jewish festival of Pentecost. As the followers of Jesus were gathered together for worship, they had an overwhelming experience of the sense of God's presence and power. And now they were quite sure that they had not lost their Master. The God whom they had known in Jesus had come into their lives far more marvellously than in the days when their Master was with them on earth, and they could now go anywhere and witness for Him. Moreover they discovered that this great new experience need not be confined to those who had known Jesus on earth. It could come to anyone, anywhere, through the story of Jesus; and so they went here and there, and told the story, and the thing kept happening, to all sorts of people. It was something new in man's knowledge of God. What was it? Was it simply Christ their Master, come back to them, unseen? Yes, and yet it was different, something more universal, something permanent. What was it? Well, these men remembered something that had been foretold by ancient prophets, and something that had been promised by their Master. And they said: the thing has come true, and now we recognize it. This is the Holy Spirit of God. God our Heavenly Father, who came to us in His Son, Jesus Christ, is with us now and for ever more, through His Holy Spirit.

And that is how Christians have come to speak of Father, Son and Holy Spirit, One God. Therefore the doctrine of the Trinity is not simply a mysterious mathematical formula of three in one. When it comes at the end of the Christian story, it sums up the *whole Gospel*, of what the Eternal God did for us in Jesus, and does for us still and to all eternity. So that the Church never tires of singing, in adoring gratitude: 'Glory be to the Father, and to the Son, and to the Holy Ghost; as it was in the beginning, is now, and ever shall be, world without end.'

I give that as an example of how even the doctrine of the Trinity, most difficult of all doctrines, can be preached to an ordinary congregation by the method of keeping close to its Biblical basis.

(*b*) The second thing I wish to say about the preaching of doctrine is that it should be related as closely as possible to the problems of daily life in our modern world. It isn't much use even being Biblical unless we see to that. It is really very difficult for us ministers who have had an elaborate theological training, and perhaps most difficult of all for us professors, to remember that the ordinary man in the pew is not interested in theology as such, and is not even interested in the Bible as a piece of ancient literature to be studied with critical commentaries. You and I have a kind of professional interest in the Bible (apart from any deeper interest), and a kind of professional interest in theological problems and controversies. But the man in the pew has neither the one nor the other, even in Scotland. If he is a good and intelligent Christian, he is deeply interested in understanding the Bible and in understanding what he believes. But it is a concrete practical interest, arising out of the problems of daily life. In that way he may sometimes put to one of us a simple pointed question about the meaning of some bit of Christian doctrine in terms of daily living, a question which brings us to the point and perhaps even pricks the bubble of some theological concept with which we had been pretty well pleased. And in that way we learn to preach doctrine concretely and practically, a far more difficult thing than to do it with the abstractions and jargon of the theological classroom, but the only kind of doctrinal preaching that is of any use to the Church.

Again I must try to give you an actual illustration. Let us suppose that in a course on Christian doctrine we have arrived at the point where we have to preach a sermon on the doctrine of providence. How should we do it?

Some years ago a very able student of our College suddenly fell ill and died. He was the only son of parents who had lost their only other child while very young. They were poor and simple folk. The father was a half-blind ex-service man, and they were making a living by keeping a small poultry-farm. Their son was the joy and crown of their lives, and they did all they could for him. He was dux of his school, then distinguished himself in his Arts course at the University, came to St. Mary's College, was suddenly taken ill and died. A few days after the funeral I mounted a bus to go out to the country and visit his parents. There happened to come into the bus an old acquaintance, a layman, whom I hadn't seen for years—a quite untheological, even unintellectual man. He sat beside me, and presently asked me where I was going. I told him, and gave him an outline of the sad story. Suddenly he said to me: 'Now, was it God who did that, or was it the Devil?' What is the answer? There is no short and easy answer. The question can't be answered in one word. For that question, coming straight from life, and asked quite spontaneously by a plain man, plumbs the very depths, the mysterious paradoxical depths, of the Christian doctrine of providence. It just shows how real even the deepest theological questions can be to the plain man when they confront him in practice, and also how a minister in his pastoral work may be called on at any moment to use whatever theology he has.

But, to come back to our subject of preaching, what an introduction a story like that can make to a sermon on the doctrine of providence! 'Was it God, or was it the Devil, that brought about that tragedy?' Take a story like the story of Joseph in the Book of Genesis, surely one of the finest stories in the world's literature in respect of a magnificent plot. It begins with a terrible tragedy, when the boy Joseph was sold by his brothers into Egypt as a slave. But then the plot thickens and gets complicated; until at last in the most marvellous way every evil is turned into good. Joseph becomes the saviour of Egypt from famine, and the saviour of his own father and brothers, who become the ancestors of the 'peculiar people' that God had chosen to do His will in the world; so that everything worked out right in the end. Was it God or was it the Devil that sent the boy Joseph away into Egypt as a slave at the beginning? Was this thing brought about by the machinations of evil wills or by the gracious purpose of God? *Both.* You remember what Joseph's own answer to that question was in the end. He says to his brothers: 'It was not you that sent me hither, but God.' And again, 'As for you, ye thought evil against me, but God meant it for good.' That is the true answer to the question that my friend asked; and if it is explained concretely, it is an answer that can be grasped by quite simple souls and that will help them to face the actual vicissitudes of their own lives in the right and Christian way; which is the real meaning of the doctrine of providence.

But perhaps it may be said that the *full* meaning of the belief in providence does not appear until we come to the New Testament; and therefore we may wish to take a New Testament text for our sermon on that subject. Well, there is one passage which seems almost made to answer my lay friend's question—the passage in Second Corinthians where St. Paul speaks of his chronic malady, the 'thorn in his flesh'. Was it God or was it the Devil that sent that painful malady to St. Paul? He tells us himself that it was *both*. Somehow both God and the Devil sent it, though for different reasons and with different purposes. He speaks of it as 'the messenger (or angel) of Satan to buffet me'. It was an evil thing, and it came from the kingdom of evil; it was the work of the power of darkness; which is just how we find our Lord speaking about suffering and disease in the Gospels. St. Paul did not pretend that suffering in itself was a good thing. What real sufferer could? *But* he faced it in a Christian way, with faith and prayer, and he got an answer. It was not the answer he had wished for, but he accepted it, and he presently came to see that it was something much better than he had wished for, because now the grace of God was using his suffering to make him spiritually a stronger man. And now in telling the story he can even *begin* with God. 'There was *given* to me a thorn in the flesh. . . .' Given by whom? Of course he means that it was given him by God, who can use even the effects of the kingdom of evil and make them work for good to them that love Him. That is the Christian doctrine of providence.

I believe that what first led or drove men to the full, rich, high Christian doctrine of providence was the episode of Calvary, the crucifixion of Jesus Christ. Was it God that did that dreadful thing? Or was it the Devil? The New Testament is quite realistic in saying that it was the forces of evil that did it—the mob that cried 'Crucify Him', and the Jewish leaders who incited them, and Pontius Pilate, and Judas Iscariot, and behind all that the Devil, who put it into the heart of Judas, and indeed the mysterious cosmic powers of darkness, the 'princes of this age' who 'crucified the Lord of glory'. And yet somehow behind *all* was the 'determinate counsel and foreknowledge of God', His infinitely gracious purpose of redemption. So that they could say with a lyrical note of joy: 'God commendeth His own love towards us, in that, while we were yet sinners, Christ died for us.' That is where the doctrine of providence passes into the doctrine of reconciliation and redemption. But even these mysteries are not too high to be declared and explained to our people from the pulpit. And how can we preach the Gospel without them?

Index of Names

🙘